KEEPING

OFF THE

CASUALTY

LIST

KEEPING OFF
THE CASUALTY
LIST

Leroy Eims

This book is designed for your personal reading pleasure and profit. It is also designed for group study. A Leader's Guide with helps and hints for teachers and with visual aids (Victor Multiuse Transparency Masters) is available from your local bookstore or from the publisher.

VICTOR

BOOKS a division of SP Publications, Inc.
WHEATON, ILLINOIS 60187

Offices also in
Whitby, Ontario, Canada
Amersham-on-the-Hill, Bucks, England

Unless otherwise noted, Bible quotations are from the *King James Version*. Other quotations are from *The Holy Bible, New International Version* (NIV), © 1973, 1978, 1984, International Bible Society. Used by permission of Zondervan Bible Publishers; and *The New Testament in Modern English*, Revised Edition, (PH), © J.B. Phillips, 1958, 1960, 1972, permission of Macmillan Publishing Company and Collins Publishers.

Recommended Dewey Decimal Classification: 248.25
Suggested Subject Headings: CHRISTIAN LIVING, MORAL REARMAMENT

Library of Congress Catalog Card Number: 85-062706
ISBN: 0-89693-152-8

C O N T E N T S

D E D I C A T I O N

To Dr. Walter Smyth, whose leadership on the Billy Graham team and steadfast walk with Christ have been a challenge to thousands around the world—and whose wise counsel, given to me when I was a young Christian worker, I have prized over the years.

PART

There's a War On

One

THE BATTLE

It was a tragic sight. Hundreds of automobiles of all shapes and sizes had been tossed helter-skelter, creating a scrap heap of mammoth proportions. Once each of those automobiles had held great promise, providing reliable transportation and pleasure for its owner. There had been trips to Grandma and Grandpa's place, vacations, commutes to work, forays to music lessons and football games. In hundreds of ways these cars had been used to make life a bit easier, more pleasant, and more efficient—but no more. They had been thrown away, becoming rusted-out hunks of unsightly junk.

As I drove past the wrecking yard, my mind shifted to another scene. I saw people, all kinds of people with marvelous potential for good and for God. They had been used by the Holy Spirit to bear testimony for Christ, to pray, to "speak a word in season to him that is weary" (Isa. 50:4). But no more. Something had happened along the way, and now they were no longer useful to God. Their testimonies had been silenced; their prayer lives had ground to a halt. Their walks with God were just memories.

Most of us know people like this. Once they were active in church, perhaps part of a lively Sunday School class, showing great spiritual promise. Now they stay home Sunday mornings to wash their cars or mow their lawns. When they are invited to church rallies or special services, they "all with one accord" begin to make excuses. The fire of their Christian lives burns so low it can scarcely be detected.

Should this surprise us? No. It should grieve us, cause us concern, alert us to search our own hearts and check our own walks with the Lord to make sure things are right. But when God's Word repeatedly alerts us to the intensity of the spiritual battle that rages around us, we should not be surprised when there are casualties.

NO DEMILITARIZED ZONE

History tells us that warfare has always produced casualties. I doubt there's ever been a war in which someone didn't fall to a crossbow, bullet, bomb, bayonet, or other destructive force. When battles are fought, people get hurt.

The Christian life *is* a battle. The New Testament practically crackles with military jargon. Paul had "fought a good fight" (2 Tim. 4:7). He admonished Timothy to "fight the good fight of faith" (1 Tim. 6:12) and spoke of certain prophecies by which Timothy might "war a good warfare" (1 Tim. 1:18). Then he added, "Thou therefore endure hardness, as a good soldier of Jesus Christ. No man that warreth entangleth himself with the affairs of this life; that he may please him who hath chosen him to be a soldier (2 Tim. 2:3, 4).

To the Corinthians Paul spoke of "the armor of righteousness" (2 Cor. 6:7). The Thessalonians were told, "But let us, who are of the day, be sober, putting on the breastplate of faith and love; and for an helmet, the hope of salvation"

(1 Thes. 5:8). And to the Ephesians he spelled out the fight in detail:

> For we wrestle not against flesh and blood, but against principalities, against powers, against the rulers of the darkness of this world, against spiritual wickedness in high places. Wherefore take unto you the whole armor of God, that ye may be able to withstand in the evil day, and having done all, to stand. Stand therefore, having your loins girt about with truth, and having on the breastplate of righteousness; and your feet shod with the preparation of the gospel of peace; above all, taking the shield of faith, wherewith ye shall be able to quench all the fiery darts of the wicked. And take the helmet of salvation, and the sword of the Spirit, which is the Word of God: praying always with all prayer and supplication in the Spirit, and watching thereunto with all persever-ance and supplication for all saints; and for me, that utterance may be given unto me, that I may open my mouth boldly, to make known the mystery of the Gos-pel, for which I am an ambassador in bonds: that therein I may speak boldly, as I ought to speak (Eph. 6:12-20).

It is obvious from all this that a spiritual war is on, and we are up to our necks in it. There is no point in trying to retreat or find a place in the rear echelon. The safest place for us is at the front line, with the captain of our salvation guiding our every move. Danger is the order of the day, but there is safety in the Lord.

THE ENEMY

One day when our son Randy was about seven years old, he was playing with neighbor kids in a backyard up the street.

Suddenly the little dog that accompanied the children began to bark. But it wasn't just a bark. It was a combination of howl, whine, and bark punctuated with yips and yelps. It was strange, different.

The mother of some of the kids went out to investigate and found a rattlesnake had slithered into the yard! But it wasn't just a rattlesnake. It was an *old, big, fat, long* rattlesnake. The dog was going bananas as the children gathered around to see the serpent. Wisely the mom herded the kids into the house and called her husband, who came and disposed of the snake.

The Apostle John has warned us about a more dangerous "old serpent" (Rev. 12:9) who began his attack on the human race in the Garden of Eden. He is the enemy, and some Christians are on the casualty list due to his assaults. Paul himself saw this happen in his ministry, as he reminded Timothy: "This thou knowest, that all they which are in Asia be turned away from me; of whom are Phygellus and Hermogenes" (2 Tim. 1:15). Note that these two did not necessarily turn their backs on the teachings of Christ, but on Paul. Perhaps they retained their faith, but their usefulness had been impaired or lost.

Haven't we all seen that happen? Someone comes into the church and becomes active for a while. Then for some reason he becomes dormant, cools off. When you speak to him, he readily acknowledges his faith; he still believes. He has no quarrel with the Bible; he thinks the pastor is a nice guy and the people in the pews are OK. But he is a casualty nevertheless. His usefulness to God's kingdom is gone.

Why do people become useless? Some fizzle out when perseverence is required. They just can't be bothered to carry their fair share of responsibility; it seems too much of a burden.

Or they begin to advance in their professions. They get

promotions, bigger salaries, fancier cars. They move to bigger houses in snootier neighborhoods and make new friends. They begin to hesitate to be involved with the plain folk who drive plain cars and live in plain, little houses in plain, little neighborhoods. So they quietly withdraw and take up new lifestyles that no longer include the Lord and His people.

GIVING UP

The writer to the Hebrews suggests another reason for casualties: "Wherefore lift up the hands which hang down, and the feeble knees; and make straight paths for your feet, lest that which is lame be turned out of the way; but let it rather be healed" (Heb. 12:12-13).

Picture a warrior on the field of battle. He is armed with shield and sword, but there is a problem: his arms hang limply at his sides and his knees are ready to buckle. Discouragement has crushed his spirit. He has forgotten the admonition, "For consider Him that endured such contradiction of sinners against Himself, lest ye be wearied and faint in your minds" (Heb. 12:3). He has taken his eyes off Christ, dwelling instead on the problems, heartaches, and pressures of life.

A weary, discouraged soldier isn't of much use, no matter how good his weapons are. Properly used, the shield of faith can quench the fiery darts of despair, and the sword of the Spirit can send the enemy into retreat. But surrender to the debilitating power of doubt and discouragement makes shield and sword just so much dead weight.

Not all Christians give up when they face hardships and difficulties, of course. Some press on regardless, while others fall away. Those who press on in the power of the Spirit of God are strengthened by the experience.

Strange, isn't it? That which strengthens some weakens others. The difference is the way we respond. But a proper response does not come out of the blue; it is usually based on a solid foundation of everyday faithfulness in the basics of the Christian life.

There is too much at stake to permit yourself to become a casualty, to be bogged down on a sidetrack. Your usefulness to God depends on your walk of faith. Others who might be walking weakly and lamely can also be challenged by your example to take courage, to turn their eyes on Jesus and follow Him.

DEFECTION AND DISILLUSIONMENT

Jesus faced the disappointment of His followers' defection. This is clearly brought to our attention by the Apostle John's statement: "From that time many of His disciples went back, and walked no more with Him" (John 6:66).

Why did they turn away? It had become clear to them that following Christ didn't mean what they'd first thought. They had not foreseen Jesus' "hard sayings," which were too much for them to handle. So they left Him, returning to the concerns that had occupied their empty lives before they had walked with Him.

This incident in the life of our Lord points out more than the fact of defections. It reminds us that we must be "right up front" about the Christian life when we urge people to surrender to the Lord. We mustn't paint a false picture, leading others to believe that receiving Christ means that all their troubles are over. We know from experience that Christians are not immune to the normal vicissitudes of life.

My friend Walt Henrichsen and I had this truth brought home to us several years ago. We spent a week together talking about Christ at colleges and universities. One night after we presented the Gospel, a professor stood to his feet and asked a question: If he became a Christian, would all his troubles dissolve?

Our answer: No.

Would he be spared from sickness or disease?

Our answer: No.

After a few more questions like those, he said, "Then what's the use? Why come to Christ? Christians are no better off than non-Christians."

He was wrong, of course, and his comment gave us a perfect opportunity to describe the Christian life. Some came to Christ as a result of that meeting, and they did it with a clear understanding of what it meant to take that step. They knew something of what they could expect in their new lives. So while we cannot anticipate every problem—nor should we try—we must not purposely paint a false picture for the sake of getting decisions.

Recognizing the possibility of defections can help us deal with them. The Apostle Paul informed Timothy, "The Spirit speaketh expressly, that in the latter times some shall depart from the faith" (1 Tim. 4:1). Paul's intent? Surely it wasn't to discourage Timothy. But Timothy was to prepare to meet these defections that the Holy Spirit had revealed to Paul. It was important enough that the Spirit had spoken "expressly" to Paul about it.

A TALE OF TWO CASUALTIES

Another cause of casualites which deserves mention is bitterness. One lady in a Sunday School class, for example, had been vitally involved—even serving as a class officer. But one Sunday morning the teacher touched on a subject that bothered this woman's conscience. She was offended by the teacher's remarks, which began to eat at her contentment.

She continued to come to class, but her attitude changed.

Whenever there was the slightest cause for complaint, she found it. The teacher sensed her displeasure and tried to make peace, but to no avail; the woman developed a bitter spirit against him and it grew to mammoth proportions. Eventually she stopped coming to class; after a few months she stopped coming to church. The devil had used bitterness to win the day.

Then there was a man who was a good Bible teacher. He taught as a substitute in various Sunday School classes and was quite popular with all of them. One day it was announced that the teacher of one of the largest and most prestigious classes in the church was leaving town, and the search for a successor was beginning.

The substitute really wanted the job. He subtly let a few people know he was available and had high hopes of being chosen. But the teaching post went to another.

The substitute became angry. *I should have been selected*, he thought. He kept coming to class for a while, but then his attendance became irregular. Finally he left the class—and the church—and as far as I know is spending his days nursing his damaged ego and wounded pride. Again the devil had used bitterness to shunt a very useful life onto a dead-end road.

Bitterness, materialism, discouragement—these and many other problems can lead to uselessness in the work of Christ. But there are time-tested preventatives that the Spirit of God can use to keep us motivated and off the casualty list. We are about to examine, chapter by chapter, causes of uselessness and solutions that are in line with the Word of God. We will look at three prime problems, how they strike people of God who are in various stages of growth, and what can be done to combat them.

Understanding the enemy is our first step. After all, there's a war on—and we're right in the middle of it.

Two

THE WORLD

It was awesome. There we were, high in the Colorado Rockies, looking down on a carpet of gold. Thousands and thousands of acres of gold aspen leaves shimmered in the September sunlight. At every bend in the trail a spectacular new sight was revealed—each one, it seemed, more beautiful than the last. At times we felt literally immersed in a golden world. Clearly God's handiwork was revealed in that sea of gold, and we loved it.

As we drove home down Ute Pass that day we began to play a little memory game. We recalled other times, other places that conjured up scenes of grandeur. In just a few minutes our minds were replaying a Hawaiian sunset, the beauty of Milford Sound in New Zealand, the steaming Indonesian jungle viewed from the window of the train between Djakarta and Bandung, and the Mediterranean Sea vista from the palace at Monaco. All were spectacular scenes of beauty which God had allowed us to behold.

We had also fallen in love with some man-made wonders. We reflected on the Cypress Gardens of Florida, the terraced rice fields of Indonesia, the Louvre, the pyramids of Mexico, Disneyland, Buckingham Palace, and the Lincoln Memorial.

As we neared our house I wondered aloud how our fondness for earthly beauty squared with the admonition of the Apostle John to "Love not the world, neither the things that are in the world" (1 John 2:15). Was it sin to be awestruck by the aspen, bowled over by Buckingham Palace, and mesmerized by the magnificence of the Mediterranean? Was this the "world" against which John had warned us so forcefully?

We didn't settle the question that day, but an examination of Scripture should provide an answer.

THE WORLD ORDER

John's word for "world" is the Greek *kosmos*, which means "a harmonious relationship." That seems to convey the idea of being "orderly."

In the beginning God created an ordered world. He placed in it a man and woman, intending that everything and everyone should reflect His grace and glory. But one look at today's headlines shows that this world has rebelled against its Creator. The problem began in the Garden of Eden when Adam sinned, as Paul tells us: "By one man sin entered into the world" (Rom. 5:12). Paul adds, "By one man's disobedience many were made sinners" (Rom. 5:19). At that point God's ordered world became disordered, caught in the viselike grip of the devil.

The Apostle John tells us, "The whole world is under the control of the evil one" (1 John 5:19, NIV). Because of this, when John speaks of the world, it has an evil overtone. It is not the world as God created it, but the world that persists in disobeying God. It is not the golden aspens or the Lincoln Memorial; it is the corrupted world system, the present evil age.

It was into *this* world that God sent His Son, "Who gave Himself for our sins, that He might deliver us from this present evil world, according to the will of God and our Father: To whom be glory forever and ever. Amen" (Gal. 1:4-5).

Two characteristics of man in "this present evil world" are pride and covetousness. Proud man is unwilling to accept the fact that he is a created being; he wants to be the measure of all things. He wants to be perfectly free to do his own thing, to live any way he pleases. Thus he concocts his personal code of right and wrong, declaring that whatever feels good to him is right. Is it any wonder that God's intended order has been ravaged and disordered, that chaos and confusion are the "order" of the day?

In his covetousness, man has an inborn drive to possess whatever pleases his physical senses. This, Paul says, is idolatry (Col. 3:5). Things that might not be wrong in themselves (like the Mediterranean or Disneyland) become wrong when more affection is riveted on them than is given to things above. "If ye then be risen with Christ, seek those things which are above, where Christ sitteth on the right hand of God. Set your affection on things above, not on things on the earth" (Col. 3:1-2).

THE SPIRIT OF THIS WORLD

In 1 Corinthians 2:12, Paul speaks of "the spirit of the world." This world has a spirit of its own, and the only way the human race can be delivered from the bondage of this spirit is to be set free by Jesus Christ—whose kingdom is not of this world. "If the Son therefore shall make you free, ye shall be free indeed" (John 8:36). When we turn to Christ in repentance and faith, we are born again and released from the sins of pride and covetousness.

John tells us, "For whatsoever is born of God overcometh the world: and this is the victory that overcometh the world, even our faith. Who is he that overcometh the world, but he that believeth that Jesus is the Son of God?" (1 John 5:4-5). We can only overcome the spirit of this world when Jesus Christ reigns in our lives. "Ye are of God, little children, and have overcome them: because greater is He that is in you, than he that is in the world" (1 John 4:4). Only when we are submitted to the lordship of Christ are we able to overcome the pride and covetousness that run rampant in this world.

It's clear from these Scriptures that our own determination won't overcome the spirit of this world nor our love for its attractions. Anemic substitutes—such as performing religious rituals, submitting to the cold power of legalism, practicing asceticism, or isolating ourselves—won't work. We can only overcome the world through what one writer called the "expulsive power of a new affection." Love for God overcomes love for this world.

Love for God also leads the disciple of Christ to march into this present world with the message of the Gospel, in obedience to Christ's command: "Go ye into all the world, and preach the Gospel to every creature" (Mark 16:15). A disciple-soldier's love for Christ helps him see this present world as it really is—not something to be desired, not something to which to conform, but a world that needs the healing and cleansing touch of Christ. The Christian can march into the world with the confidence of victory, knowing that one day every knee that now bows to the spirit of this world will one day bow to Christ: "That every tongue should confess that Jesus Christ is Lord, to the glory of God the Father" (Phil. 2:11). He can look forward to the day when "The kingdoms of this world are become the kingdoms of our Lord, and of His Christ; and He shall reign forever and ever" (Rev. 11:15).

THE SAD CASE OF DEMAS

In the meantime, there is Demas. I wish I'd never heard of him. But there he is in the Bible, a constant reminder of the drawing power of this world.

Despite the matter-of-fact way Paul describes Demas' defection in 2 Timothy, I believe there was a mighty ache in the apostle's heart: "For Demas hath forsaken me, having loved this present world, and is departed unto Thessalonica" (2 Tim. 4:10). Demas had been Paul's coworker, mentioned with other notables like Mark, Aristarchus, and Luke (Phile. 24). Demas, a trained soldier of the cross, was now a deserter.

To what did he desert? What entered his heart and caused him to turn aside? The world. Probably not the whole, elaborate, tinsel-filled world—not at first. But somehow a small seed of pride or covetousness took root, and grew. It grew steadily, secretly, until it began to dominate his thinking. Finally it took over. Desire and opportunity met; Demas packed up and headed for the things of *this* life. He would probably find this verse offensive: "Thou therefore endure hardness, as a good soldier of Jesus Christ. No man that warreth entangleth himself with the affairs of this life; that he may please him who hath chosen him to be a soldier" (2 Tim. 2:3-4).

Did Demas find the happiness he expected? We are not told. But there are Scriptures that lead me to believe he didn't. Note, for instance, 1 Timothy 6:9-10: "But they that will be rich fall into temptation and a snare, and into many foolish and hurtful lusts, which drown men in destruction and perdition. For the love of money is the root of all evil: which while some coveted after, they have erred from the faith, and pierced themselves through with many sorrows."

Paul is not speaking here of the rich. He has advice for them later in verses 17 and 18. Here he is admonishing those who *desire* riches—whose hearts are set on the things of this world. He refers to money-hunger as a snare, something that trips and entangles us. The worldly person is lured by the bait, trapped, and held fast. Greed hurts, and the hurt is not just temporal. There are eternal consequences.

MONEY, PLEASURE, AND THE "GOOD LIFE"

Love of money plays a part in many cautionary Bible accounts. One thinks of Judas and his thirty pieces of silver. Then there was a "certain rich man, which was clothed in purple and fine linen, and fared sumptuously every day" (Luke 16:19). His appetite was denied nothing money could buy; his wardrobe was unmatched; his life was one party after another. After he died, he found himself in hell.

But we might ask, "What harm is there in wearing good clothes and eating good food? Is it a sin to be rich?"

No, not exactly. The richest man I know is also one of the most dedicated, generous, and godly. His life is Christ-centered; he is a powerful witness. Money has not hurt him a bit. God's blessing is on his fruitful life.

As far as we know, the man in Christ's story did not get his wealth by making crooked deals and oppressing his business associates. His problem was simple. He had been blinded by the things of this world to the realities of life. His plenty and pleasures made him forget God. His sin was not so much in having clothes and food, but in letting the spirit of this world lure him into thinking only of Himself.

No, riches in themselves are not a curse. Abraham, mentioned also in the Luke story, was also a wealthy man—and he was faring well in the afterlife. But the "certain rich man" was a perfect picture of Paul's words in Philippians 3:18-19: "For many walk, of whom I have told you often, and now tell you even weeping, that they are the enemies of the cross of

Christ: Whose end is destruction, whose God is their belly, and whose glory is in their shame, who mind earthly things." James paints the same picture with different words: "Ye adulterers and adulteresses, know ye not that the friendship of the world is enmity with God? Whosoever therefore will be a friend of the world is the enemy of God" (James 4:4). In other places this is called idolatry; here it is called adultery. Like an unfaithful spouse, the defector has left the Lord and taken up with the world.

The Prophet Jeremiah records a warning concerning this "change of gods":

> "Wherefore I will yet plead with you," saith the Lord, "and with your children's children will I plead. For pass over the isles of Chittim, and see; and send unto Kedar, and consider diligently, and see if there be such a thing. Hath a nation changed their gods, which are yet no gods? But My people have changed their glory for that which doth not profit. Be astonished, O ye heavens, at this, and be horribly afraid, be ye very desolate," saith the Lord. "For My people have committed two evils; they have forsaken Me the fountain of living waters, and hewed them out cisterns, broken cisterns, that can hold no water" (Jer. 2:9-13).

Heaven itself is called on in this passage to observe in astonishment such a foolish and sinful desertion. Why did God not call on the earth as well? Because the earth is so universally corrupt it would probably see nothing wrong! The spirit of this world would probably applaud the defectors' actions. But the angels of God, who rejoice when people repent and turn to Him, are no doubt astonished and afraid to see people turn their backs on Him. Imagine trading the everlasting, all-sufficient fountain of living waters for broken cisterns. The thirsty person coming to those reservoirs would find nothing but smelly sediment. The trade is reckless—and dangerous.

If we try to find happiness in wealth and pleasure, we will find them to be cracked cisterns. They look fine on the outside, but the world's ability to deceive is well known. As Jesus said, "The world cannot hate you; but Me it hateth, because I testify of it, that the works thereof are evil" (John 7:7).

The Psalmist also knew that the "good life" is not found in material things: "There be many that say, Who will show us any good? Lord, lift Thou up the light of Thy countenance upon us. Thou hast put gladness in my heart, more than in the time that their corn and their wine increased" (Ps. 4:6-7). Here we see world-bound people inquiring into the good life, wanting an increase of corn and wine. But David sees it differently; he wants the blessing of God. He finds the good life in his fellowship with the Lord.

IT'S NOT EASY

Four young men once formed a singing group. They were all students at a Christian college, and all were committed to serving the Lord. Excellent musicians, they soon gained a reputation that stretched far and wide.

One evening a man who was affiliated with a national TV musical variety show heard them at a Christian concert. He offered them an audition, and they accepted—assuring each other that this opportunity might open a wider door for witness. Much to their delight and surprise, they won a spot on the show and became quite popular.

Soon those men were performing in the finest resorts, and nightclubs, and concert halls. Little by little their basic motivation changed. Instead of watching for opportunities to witness, they began to look for ways to enhance their careers. Often performing on weekends and late Saturday nights, they began to skip church and sleep in on Sunday mornings. The glitter and glamour of the world dazzled them; parties and "life in the fast lane" soon dominated their desires.

As the members pressed on toward material success, they completely dropped church, Bible reading, and Christian fellowship. The world had drawn them into a web that held them fast, and their Christian values died a slow but sure death.

Resisting the lure of this world is not easy. The system is always at us, trying to squeeze us into its mold and set our minds on its own values. No halfhearted resistance on our part will give us victory; drastic measures are called for. Paul states the solution clearly and simply: We must be crucified to the world and the world must be crucified to us (Gal. 2:20; 6:14). A double crucifixion! The cross of Christ must be our chief glory, for it is to the crucified and risen Christ that we owe our joy in this life and our hope for eternity.

But keeping this perspective is difficult. Just how difficult it is was brought to my attention recently when my wife and I attended a Parade of Homes to see the latest marvels in architecture. About a dozen homes were on display, and they were beautiful. As we walked from one to another I found myself thinking, *Wouldn't it be great to live in a home like these? Think of the way I could enhance the ministry. Think how nice it would be to have a kitchen with all these modern, time-saving gadgets and conveniences. Wouldn't it be great to have this lovely view, this elaborate recreation room complete with a giant hot tub?*

As we were leaving, my wife jarred me back to reality by telling me she'd read in a missionary newsletter that some Christian brothers and sisters in Asia have no homes at all. I found myself thanking God for the home we have and asking His forgiveness for my lapse into unspiritual daydreaming.

Yes, this world is attractive, and none of us is immune to its pull. But we have the key to victory. It lies not in comparing our lot with those less fortunate, but in keeping before us the lifestyle of the Lord Jesus. He had no place to lay His head. "Though He was rich, yet for your sakes He became poor, that ye through His poverty might be rich" (2 Cor. 8:9). He left the mansions of heaven and chose life as a servant to others in this sin-cursed world.

Paul was dead to the things of the world. The power of Christ had weaned him from that system. The world had no liking for Paul, and he had no great admiration for the world; he lived above its flattery and frowns as a man who was dead. This should be our mindset, and the quickest way to attain it is to spend time at the foot of the Cross. The greater our love for Christ, the smaller will be our opinion of this world's glare and glitter. The more we think on His sufferings, the less likely we are to wind up on the casualty list. Crucifixion is tough, but it is the only sure way to victory in this war.

I am crucified with Christ: nevertheless I live; yet not I, but Christ liveth in me: and the life which I now live in the flesh I live by the faith of the Son of God, who loved me, and gave Himself for me (Gal. 2:20).

Three

THE FLESH

That old saying, "War is hell," is probably an overstatement. When we read what Jesus said about hell, nothing could compare. But the statement does convey the truth that war is horrible, dangerous, brutal, terrifying. People get hurt in wars; hearts break in loneliness. Homesickness runs rampant; a letter from home is read until it is worn thin. And, of course, people die.

As a young Marine wounded in World War II, I experienced most of these things. I learned firsthand the harsh realities of a global war that became very personal. I learned that the best thing about war is that it eventually ends; if you survive you can relax, let down your guard, get a good night's sleep, celebrate, and eventually go home to mom and dad.

But there is one war that never seems to end. Peter spoke of this conflict when he said, "Dearly beloved, I beseech you as strangers and pilgrims, abstain from fleshly lusts, which war against the soul" (1 Peter 2:11). Here is a war with casualties.

PRESSURES OF THE FLESH

Our study of "the flesh" begins with a close look at the aforementioned verse. Peter calls his readers strangers and pilgrims; some recent translations say "aliens and strangers in the world" (NIV) and "temporary residents" (PH). According to *An Expository Dictionary of New Testament Words* by W. E. Vine (Revell), the word *pilgrim* implies "sojourning in a strange place away from one's own people." Vine adds, "The word is thus used metaphorically of those whom heaven is their country, and who are sojourners on earth."

Just before this verse, Peter had referred to his readers as "the people of God" (v. 10) and as "a chosen people, a royal priesthood, a holy nation, a people belonging to God" (v. 9, NIV). That's a high calling indeed! Yet even the best of people with the highest of callings need Peter's warning to abstain from the pagan practices around them.

The non-Christian, a citizen of this world alone, naturally indulges the promptings of his fleshly desires. But the Christian, whose true citizenship is in heaven, is governed by a higher law. So as we sojourn in this alien world as "temporary residents," we should do nothing that would impede our ability to fight the spiritual battle. Every submission to the lust of the flesh is a step closer to the casualty list.

It can happen to anyone. One congregation, whose pastor was highly respected throughout the Christian world as a wise marriage counselor, found this to be true. One morning without warning the pastor announced that he was getting a divorce from his wife—and was going to marry the church secretary! The church was in shock, then angry. The elders tried to reason with the pastor, but to no avail; his mind was made up. It didn't matter to him how all of this would affect his wife and children, the church, or its testimony for Christ in the city. He admitted that what he was doing was contrary to what he believed and had taught others, but that made no difference. He was going to do it anyway.

His problem? Disobedience. He had caved in to the pressures of the lust of the flesh. Today he is practically useless to the kingdom of God. His actions have caused heartbreak for many of his friends, sorrow and humiliation for his family, and set up one more roadblock to the kingdom of God for many non-Christians in the area.

A SINGLE EYE

Peter describes these fleshly lusts as forces that "war against the soul." When Peter uses the word "war," he is describing not only hand-to-hand combat but also a planned campaign. The enemy maps out objectives, chooses strategy and tactics, and decides which weapons to use. This is warfare on a grand scale—truly global, yet raging in the hearts of all of us.

The enemy's ultimate objective is to capture souls, take them prisoner, enslave them, and eventually destroy them. We can compare this campaign to the biblical story of Delilah, who exploited Samson's fleshly appetites to his own downfall and eventual destruction. She did not act willy-nilly, but followed a well-thought-out plan to ruin the man. This is the kind of war about which Peter is warning.

One of the most powerful protections we have in this war is to remember that this world is not our home—to see our days as preparation for heaven. Abraham is an excellent example:

"By faith he sojourned in the land of promise, as in a strange country, dwelling in tabernacles with Isaac and Jacob, the heirs with him of the same promise: For he looked for a city which hath foundations, whose builder and maker is God (Heb. 11:9-10).

Abraham was a sojourner, a pilgrim with his eyes fixed on eternity. He lived in tents as an outsider, placing his faith in things hoped for but not seen. His affections were set on things above, not on the things of this earth. His focus relates to the prayer of Dawson Trotman, founder of The Navigators: "God, give us a band of rugged soldiers of the Cross with an eye single to your glory."

As Jesus taught, "The light of the body is the eye: if therefore thine eye be single, thy whole body shall be full of light. But if thine eye be evil, thy whole body shall be full of darkness. If therefore the light that is in thee be darkness, how great is that darkness!" (Matt. 6:22-23)

As we sojourn in this alien world, we will not be trapped by the desires of the flesh if we follow the example of Abraham and the admonition of Christ.

THE WORKS OF THE FLESH

When Peter speaks of the flesh, he is referring to man's lower nature, devoid of the Spirit of God, dominated by sensual appetites. Paul elaborates in Ephesians 2:3: "Among whom also we all had our conversation in times past in the lusts of our flesh, fulfilling the desires of the flesh and of the mind; and were by nature the children of wrath, even as others." Here is a person taken captive—a slave to his corrupt, filthy mind and his lower nature. This is a frightening thought when we remember the comment of Paul: "For I know that in me (that is, in my flesh), dwelleth no good thing: for to will is present with me; but how to perform that which is good I find not" (Rom. 7:18). Think of it: Dominated by a force which has no redeeming value, serving the law of sin (Rom. 7:25). Man's unregenerate, fleshly nature provides a perfect place for sin to dwell.

Paul sheds additional light in this conflict that rages in us: "For the flesh lusteth against the Spirit, and the Spirit against the flesh: and these are contrary the one to the other: so that ye cannot do the things that ye would" (Gal. 5:17). The flesh has cravings of its own (Eph. 2:3), and here we see it in a giant tug-of-war with the Holy Spirit. They are locked in a lifelong battle, with the Holy Spirit working to keep us from doing things we would probably do if left on our own.

If we want victory over the flesh, we must place ourselves under the leadership of the Holy Spirit. He wants to control our lives in order to lead us into the abundant life in Christ. This can only happen if the Spirit is not hampered or grieved by sin in our lives. That is why we are admonished, "And grieve not the holy Spirit of God, whereby ye are sealed unto the day of redemption" (Eph. 4:30). The best antidote for the poison of sin is to walk in the power and fullness of the Holy Spirit. That's why Paul says, "This I say then, Walk in the Spirit, and ye shall not fulfill the lust of the flesh" (Gal. 5:16).

What happens when the lust of the flesh is fulfilled? Paul minces no words as he spells out the results of failing to walk in the Spirit:

Now the works of the flesh are manifest, which are these; adultery, fornication, uncleanness, lasciviousness, idolatry, witchcraft, hatred, variance, emulations, wrath, strife, seditions, heresies, envyings, murders, drunken-ness, revelings, and such like: of the which I tell you before, as I have also told you in time past, that they which do such things shall not inherit the kingdom of God (Gal. 5:19-21).

These are the accomplishments of the flesh—the products of man's depraved nature. He says these are "manifest," or on public display. They result when the flesh is in control.

WORK #1: ADULTERY

The first work of the flesh Paul mentions is adultery. This is an act of sexual immorality with another person's spouse. It is the willful violation of the marriage vow to remain faithful. It is a violation of the seventh commandment: "Thou shalt not commit adultery" (Ex. 20:14). But Jesus took the matter a step further:

> Ye have heard that it was said by them of old time, Thou shalt not commit adultery: But I say unto you, That whosoever looketh on a woman to lust after her hath committed adultery with her already in his heart. And if thy right eye offend thee, pluck it out, and cast it from thee: for it is profitable for thee that one of thy members should perish, and not that thy whole body should be cast into hell (Matt. 5:27-29).

Adultery is deeper than the physical act. Jesus condemned even the glance that is prompted by lust, which helps us see that the source of sin lies in the heart. Therefore the heart of man must be changed if he is to escape the final punishment of hell. To the one who complains that he couldn't help what he did, trying to blame the whole thing on his lustful eye, Jesus says, "Get rid of it."

I saw such a severe cure in action while I recovered from a combat wound in a naval hospital on Guadalcanal during World War II. Doctors did not hesitate to amputate a man's gangrenous leg; it was the only way to save his life. Jesus' words also convey something of the awfulness of adultery.

WORK #2: FORNICATION

Fornication is mentioned next in Paul's list. The definition of this sin is broader than adultery, including illicit sexual acts in or out of marriage. Interestingly, the Greek word here is *pornea*, from which we get the word "pornography." In Acts 15, when the Council of Jerusalem met to suggest basic behavioral guidelines for Gentile converts without infringing on their Christian liberty, James included this sin as one that must be avoided:

> Wherefore my sentence is, that we trouble not them, which from among the Gentiles are turned to God: But that we write unto them, that they abstain from pollutions of idols, and from fornication, and from things strangled, and from blood (Acts 15:19-20)

Paul concurs: "Flee fornication. Every sin that a man doeth is without the body; but he that committeth fornication sinneth against his own body" (1 Cor. 6:18). To "flee" is to run and keep on running, to get out as quickly as possible. Some sins may be overcome by fight; this one only by flight.

Paul told the Ephesians that this sin should be banned from their midst: "But fornication, and all uncleanness, or covetousness, let it not be once named among you, as becometh saints" (Eph. 5:3). This verse gives us some indication of how terrible this sin is. We should also put it to death: "Mortify therefore your members which are upon the earth; fornication, uncleanness, inordinate affection, evil concupiscence, and covetousness, which is idolatry" (Col. 3:5). To the Thessalonians Paul wrote, "For this is the will of God, even your sanctification, that ye should abstain from fornication" (1 Thes. 4:3).

The Apostle John lists this sin alongside murder, sorcery, and theft: "Neither repented they of their murders, nor of their sorceries, nor of their fornication, nor of their thefts" (Rev. 9:21). Western values today are much different; this sin is taken lightly. But we must be guided by the Bible.

WORK #3: UNCLEANNESS

Next on the list is the sin of uncleanness. In Greek, the word is *akathartos*. It is related to our word "catharsis," which means a purging that brings about spiritual renewal or release from tension.

Now, think with me for a moment. If we say a person is mechanically minded, we mean he is good with his hands—he can fix things. If we say he is "*a*mechanical," we mean just the opposite. So when Paul uses the word *akathartos*, he means the opposite of catharsis—not that which cleanses but that which fouls a person, making him impure in thought, speech, and action.

Today the sin of uncleanness is rampant. Even T-shirts carry lewd messages. Foul talk can be heard in most any restaurant, supermarket, post office, or gas station; it is no longer limited to bars, military barracks, or locker rooms. Uncleanness has engulfed society, threatening to break the weakened thread of our moral fabric. But Paul reminds us that "God hath not called us unto uncleanness, but unto holiness" (1 Thes. 4:7).

WORK #4: LASCIVIOUSNESS

Lasciviousness is a word that implies no restraints, like a runaway team of horses. I use that comparison because as a child I spent Saturday nights with the rest of the kids in a little motion picture theater in Neola, Iowa. We watched cowboy pictures that starred Hoot Gibson, Ken Maynard, Buck Jones, and the like. Every week on the screen some stagecoach-pulling horses would stampede. The heroine in the stagecoach would scream, and the hero would come to the rescue. Lasciviousness is a particularly dangerous stampede.

While uncleanness is like a plague, quietly spreading death

in all directions, lasciviousness is shameless conduct totally out of control. It roars along, loud, arrogant, indecent, and wanton. Paul describes those who are overcome by this sin as being "past feeling" (Eph. 4:19) and "having their conscience seared with a hot iron" (1 Tim. 4:2). Lascivious people strut through life, proud of their unbridled lust. Jesus spoke of this sin as one of those evil things that comes from within and defiles a man (Mark 7:20-23). The roots of this sin are in the fleshly nature of an evil heart, but its fruits are blatantly displayed—offensive, rude, loud, and clear.

WORK #5: IDOLATRY

The Galatians 5:20 list continues with sins of a different nature. Idolatry, a devotion to idols, is next. We tend to sweep this sin under the rug, thinking it applies only to those who worship gods of sticks and stone. But it is easy for "civilized" man to fall into this sin. Closets can be filled with idols made of dacron, silk, and wool. Garages can be stuffed with idols made of steel, baked-on enamel, tinted glass, leather upholstery, and chrome. Idols can also take the form of elaborate houses, machines that bring us music in stereo, and kitchens littered with the latest gadgets.

It is no sin to own a good car or a nice suit or to listen to pretty music. But if a craving for these things comes between God and me, then they have become idols. They become false gods, and false gods can never satisfy. Only the living, true God can do that. We can be protected from turning good, useful things into idols by reminding ourselves that the Bible refers to them as vanity and things of naught: "Gold, and precious stones, and pearls . . . in one hour so great riches is come to naught" (Rev. 18:16-17).

WORK #6: WITCHCRAFT

Next comes the word "witchcraft," which is sometimes translated "sorcery." It is the Greek word *pharmakia*, the root of our word "pharmacy." The biblical reference is to drugs and spells, accompanied by chants and appeals to the rulers of the darkness of this world—to wicked, spiritual, unseen forces.

This is another sin we often try to relegate to primitive societies. But it is rampant throughout the globe. Fortune-tellers abound; most newspapers in the Western world carry a daily horoscope reading. This is a sin that God detests:

> When thou art come into the land which the Lord thy God giveth thee, thou shalt not learn to do after the abominations of those nations. There shall not be found among you any one that maketh his son or his daughter to pass through the fire, or that useth divination, or an observer of times, or an enchanter, or a witch. Or a charmer, or a consulter with familiar spirits, or a wizard, or a necromancer. For all that do these things are an abomination unto the Lord: and because of these abominations the Lord thy God doth drive them out from before thee. Thou shalt be perfect with the Lord thy God. For these nations, which thou shalt possess, hearkened unto observers of times, and unto diviners: but as for thee, the Lord thy God hath not suffered thee so to do (Deut. 18:9-14).

Note the word "abomination." It appears three times in this passage, and the Lord uses it to convey His loathing of this sin. As stated in verse 12, "Because of these abomina tions the Lord thy God doth drive them out from before thee." These people lost everything—their homes, families, land, and lives—because they persisted in these practices.

We must be alert to warn family, friends, and neighbors who are caught in any form of witchcraft, helping them turn to the living God for life's answers.

WORK #7: HATRED

Next Paul speaks of hatred, sometimes translated "enmity." At first glance we may be surprised that Paul would place this "socially acceptable" sin alongside such "shockers" as witchcraft and immorality. But hatred is the exact opposite of Christlike, God-given love. One has only to look at the opposite side of 1 Corinthians 13 to see the misery that characterizes the life filled with enmity, hatred, and hostility: impatience, unkindness, jealousy, boastings, arrogance, and rudeness are commonplace. The hater insists on his own way, is irritable and resentful, and rejoices when someone is wronged. Hate bears nothing, believes nothing, hopes for nothing, and endures nothing. Is it any wonder Paul lists this sin as a product of the flesh?

WORK #8: VARIANCE

Next to be named is variance—meaning strife, wrangling, contention, and debate. It is the essence of a quarrelsome person. Such a person would probably be lonely because most of us shun a quarrelsome individual; he would be unhappy because, as Jesus said, "Blessed [happy] are the peacemakers" (Matt. 5:9).

The person snared by this sin is a sad case. Variance breeds ulcers, fights, separation, bitterness, intolerance, resentment—a life of constant upheaval. Paul has an interesting way of describing this person: "He is proud, knowing nothing, but doting about questions and strifes of words, whereof cometh envy, strife, railings, evil surmisings, perverse disputings of men of corrupt minds, and destitute of the truth, supposing that gain is godliness: from such withdraw thyself" (1 Tim. 6:4-5).

This sin has a devastating effect when it enters a home or church. Nothing good can come of it.

WORK #9: JEALOUSY

Jealousy appears next. It is a spirit that burns with an unfriendly excitement about someone else's good fortune and possession of nice things. Jealousy doesn't necessarily mean that we want to take away what the other person has; we just wish we had it too. It is a refusal to abide by the Scripture, "Be content with such things as ye have" (Heb. 13:5). Paul displays the biblical attitude:

"Not that I speak in respect of want: for I have learned, in whatsoever state I am, therewith to be content. I know both how to be abased, and I know how to abound: everywhere and in all things I am instructed both to be full and to be hungry, both to abound and to suffer need" (Phil. 4:11-12).

To be in the grip of this sin is to live a life of dissatisfaction. The jealous person lacks peace; his smile is infrequent; his facial muscles tense. This is definitely a work of the flesh.

WORK #10: WRATH

Another work of the flesh is wrath. It means bursts of anger, losing one's temper, flying into a rage. Before I became a Christian I was taken by this sin; I was difficult to be around because I frequently flew off the handle. I had a very short fuse, and the littlest thing would set me off.

I remember one angry episode in particular. My wife Virginia gave me a beautiful gold ring with a diamond set in black onyx. I put it on and liked it very much. But shortly after that, some event prompted me to lose my temper. I leaped to my feet and pounded my fist into a huge hardwood door, smashing the onyx. The ring was ruined.

Wrath is the work of the flesh that spawns much of the domestic violence—wife beating, child abuse—that has filled our newspapers and television reports. People are walking the streets bruised and battered because someone fell to this sin.

WORK #11: STRIFE

Strife, a word sometimes translated "faction," comes next. Here is the sin that causes us to insist on being in charge— for the wrong reasons.

Self-seeking, rivalry, excessive ambition—all these spawn division. Church splits do not always occur over false doctrine or heresy. They can come as one individual held by this sin gathers followers. When this happens, a congregation can be shattered. What a tragedy!

How painful it is to watch a body which has had a clear testimony for Christ become embroiled in strife. One church I know of had a positive influence for the Gospel in the community; many were brought to Christ. But then it happened—a nasty split. One man insisted on his point of view and eventually led a number of people out of the church. The body's testimony was nullified and has not recovered to this day. The works of the flesh are open for all to see.

WORK #12: SEDITIONS

The word "seditions" carries with it the idea of standing apart. People who have this spirit never join in. They may be *in* the church, but they are never really part of it. They are present but not really there; they accept no responsibility. They refuse to teach a class or serve on a board. They are never part of the team.

Is it possible that Paul had found people like this at Philippi? "Only let your conversation be as it becometh the Gospel of Christ: that whether I come and see you, or else be absent, I may hear of your affairs, that ye stand fast in one spirit, with one mind striving together for the faith of the Gospel" (Phil. 1:27). Were there people in Rome who were "standing apart," so that Paul felt it necessary to remind them, "None of us liveth to himself and no man dieth to himself?" (Rom. 14:7)

One thing we know for sure. The ministry that is filled with people who never give their hearts can be of little value to the advance of the Gospel.

WORK #13: HERESIES

Next come heresies. Peter also warned of this work of the flesh: "But there were false prophets also among the people, even as there shall be false teachers among you, who privily shall bring in damnable heresies, even denying the Lord that bought them, and bring upon themselves swift destruction" (2 Peter 2:1).

Heresies lead to ruin. The word implies a choice—setting forth false doctrine that leads to moral collapse. When the false teachers have completed their work, the church is a pile of rubble—just as a wrecking crew knocks down a building. How thankful those of us should be who belong to sound churches whose leaders base their actions and teachings on the Bible. This work of the flesh also reminds us to do all we can to ground ourselves and new believers in the Word and in Christ—lest we and they end up on the casualty list.

WORK #14: ENVYINGS

Galatians 5:21 starts out with "envyings." The base of this word is ill will. This ill will is prompted by the happiness or good fortune of another, and leads the person enmeshed in this sin to long for the ruin of the prosperous person. The envious person does what he can to defile, destroy, or corrupt the one who seems better off, wanting to see him shrivel up and wither away.

Paul confessed to Titus on this point, "For we ourselves also were sometimes foolish, disobedient, deceived, serving divers lusts and pleasures, living in malice and envy, hateful, and hating one another" (Titus 3:3).

WORK #15: MURDERS

Next come murders. Murder is hatred, bitterness, antagonism, suspicion, and jealousy taken to the extreme. But remember—we can destroy another with just a word spoken sarcastically. Gossip can destroy. Shunning a person can often crush his spirit. There are many ways we can "murder." Jesus added a whole new dimension to the Old Testament definition of this sin:

> Ye have heard that it was said by them of old time, Thou shalt not kill; and whosoever shall kill shall be in danger of the judgment: But I say unto you, That whosoever is angry with his brother without a cause shall be in danger of the judgment: and whosoever shall say to his brother, Raca, shall be in danger of the council: but whosoever shall say, Thou fool, shall be in danger of hellfire (Matt. 5:21-22).

The antidote to murderous feelings is a good dose of Paul's comments to the Ephesians: "With all lowliness and meekness, with long-suffering, forbearing one another in love; endeavouring to keep the unity of the Spirit in the bond of peace. . . . Let all bitterness, and wrath, and anger, and clamor, and evil speaking, be put away from you, with all malice: and be ye kind one to another, tenderhearted, forgiving one another, even as God for Christ's sake hath forgiven you" (Eph. 4:2-3, 31-32).

WORK #16: DRUNKENNESS

Two works of the flesh are left, and they are related. The first is drunkenness—habitual intoxication, being hooked on alcohol.

I have a little experience in this area. While I was growing up, drinking was a normal part of our family. My dad made home brew, and we had lots of beer around the house all the time. I never saw a family member get drunk, but I had a problem: I really liked the stuff. By the time I left home to join the Marines, I was quite a drinker. When I returned home after World War II, I was getting drunk rather regularly. My friends and I would go to Omaha and hit the bars.

What had started out as a sort of social thing turned to excess. I added hard liquor to my drinking menu; my favorite drink was a boilermaker, a shot of liquor washed down with a glass of beer. It had sort of crept up on me; I hadn't planned on being a drunk, but I was fast becoming one. As I look back on that part of my life, Proverbs 20:1 comes to mind: "Wine is a mocker, strong drink is raging: and whosoever is deceived thereby is not wise." Thank God for the Gospel by which the Lord delivered me!

WORK #17: REVELINGS

Our last word is revelings. Peter described it well:

For the time past of our life may suffice us to have wrought the will of the Gentiles, when we walked in lasciviousness, lusts, excess of wine, revelings, banquetings, and abominable idolatries: wherein they think it strange that ye run not with them to the same excess of riot, speaking evil of you: who shall give account to Him that is ready to judge the quick and the dead (1 Peter 4:3-5).

Reveling implies "letting loose." J.H. Thayer's *Greek-English Lexicon of the New Testament* (Baker) describes reveling from ancient writings: "A nocturnal and riotous procession of half drunken and frolicsome fellows who after supper parade through the streets with torches and music in honor of Bacchus or some other deity, and sing and play before the houses of their male and female friends."

So ends the list of the products of the flesh.

DON'T FEED THE FLESH

The clear promise and admonition of 2 Corinthians 6:17–7:1 is this:

"Wherefore come out from among them, and be ye separate," saith the Lord, "and touch not the unclean thing; and I will receive you, and will be a Father unto you, and ye shall be My sons and daughters," saith the Lord Almighty. Having therefore these promises, dearly beloved, let us cleanse ourselves from all filthiness of the flesh and spirit, perfecting holiness in the fear of God.

But how do we find cleansing from the filthiness of the flesh? Galatians 5:16 gives the answer: "This I say then, Walk in the Spirit, and ye shall not fulfill the lust of the flesh."

Living in the Spirit will be analyzed in Part 3 of this book, but for now one thing is evident. One of the best weapons in our battle against the flesh is simply to starve it. Paul wrote, "But put ye on the Lord Jesus Christ, and make not provision for the flesh, to fulfill the lusts thereof" (Rom. 13:14). Most movies, many television programs, magazines, and books, for example, are shot through with stories and pictures that feed the flesh. Are we seeking or avoiding such material?

I heard once about a bank robber who, in his flight from the law, holed up in a cave. The posse chasing him did not try to storm the cave; wisely, the deputies just sat down and waited for the robber's food to run out. They knew he would eventually have to surrender. If you don't feed the flesh, it will weaken to the point where it can be overcome by the Spirit. That's an important part of keeping off the casualty list.

Four

THE DEVIL

Having no information is better than having false information. That's what I was told when I worked as a depot agent for the Chicago Great Western Railroad. To give a traveler directions that put him on the wrong train going in the wrong direction can have severe consequences.

I was once the victim of false information while on a preaching tour in Asia. When I left the U.S. my travel agent said I didn't need a visa to go to Taiwan. But, when I presented my ticket to the airline in Tokyo for the flight to Taipei, I was told I couldn't go without a visa. That began a frustrating search for the Taiwanese official in Tokyo who could issue one; our taxi driver didn't have a clue where the office was, but that didn't stop him from searching. He would speed along, then stop and ask directions, then go again, down one street and up another. Finally he found the right place, but I missed the flight.

An incident in my hometown of Neola, Iowa provides another example of what can happen when false information is transmitted. Neola, population 839, is bordered by two interstate highways. When it came time for road repairs at the interchange of Interstates 80 and 680, the Iowa Department of Transportation rerouted the eastbound lanes of I-680 through Neola.

According to Will Hoover of the *Des Moines Register,* a few summertime pranksters were unable to refrain from taking advantage of the situation. They removed a single bolt from a directional arrow and aimed it the opposite way, sending eastbound I-680 traffic streaming up Second Street and into the driveway of a Neola resident. "It was about midnight," the resident recalled later. "There were at least 10 or 15 eighteen-wheelers [large semi-trucks] and I don't know how many cars. There was no place for them to go once they got here. We just couldn't figure out what was going on." The man spent much of the night unsnarling the massive trafic jam before he found time to fix the reversed directional sign.

Undaunted, the pranksters nailed a "Wrong Way—Do Not Enter" sign to a post near the tracks on Highway 244, which resulted in eastbound I-680 traffic "meandering down side streets and every which way" according to an observer. Highway officials finally got things back to normal, but in the meantime false information had caused chaos.

In the spiritual realm, wrong information can put Christians on the casualty list. A recent missionary prayer letter told of an unusually gifted young man who had walked closely with the Lord for over eight years. This man is now in tremendous danger from the influence of false teachers and false doctrine. None of us is immune.

Behind all the false doctrine and false teachers in the world lurks one person: the devil. Peter warns, "Be sober, be vigilant; because your adversary the devil, as a roaring lion, walketh about, seeking whom he may devour" (1 Peter 5:8). In our spiritual combat with the devil, a calm and collected spirit, along with an alert and circumspect mind, is a must. His attacks are powerful yet often very subtle.

It is sometimes difficult to sort through the mass of material that comes our way in print, on television, on cassette tape, and from the pulpit—and to clearly discern its truthfulness. Dawson Trotman once asked, "Which is more dangerous—a doctrine that is 90 percent truth with 10 percent error, or one that is 10 percent truth and 90 percent error?" Perhaps the one with 10 percent error is more dangerous, because it is harder to spot. Either way, falsehood can be clothed in truth.

THE PLUMB LINE

An alert mind is not the complete answer to discerning false doctrine. We must also be grounded in the truth of Scripture. Then we can hold doctrine up to the light of God's Word.

The fact that God has made His Word available to His people is evidence of His great care and love. What an unspeakable privilege it is to have the very Word of God to guide us into all truth! Isaiah spells it out: "Bind up the testimony, seal the law among my disciples. . . . To the law and to the testimony: if they speak not according to this word, it is because there is no light in them" (Isa. 8:16, 20).

God's Word is testimony and law, and as such must be preserved accurately. The testimony of the Word feeds our faith; as law it gives clear guidelines to our walk in fellowship with the Lord. This Word is bound and sealed; nothing must be added or taken away. It is like the sealed envelopes at the Academy Awards, arriving unchanged by any outside influence.

The Bible's value is attested to by the most reliable witness of all—God Himself. As disciples of Christ, we have these Scriptures committed to us as a sacred deposit. Paul's word to Timothy applies to us as well: "Hold fast the form of sound words, which thou hast heard of me, in faith and love which is in Christ Jesus. That good thing which was committed unto thee keep by the Holy Ghost which dwelleth in us" (2 Tim. 1:13-14).

In God's Word we will discover what is good, what He expects of us. When we make God's Word our counselor, we will not be led astray by false teachers. These wolves in sheep's clothing can be spotted through a simple test: Do they teach according to the truth of Scripture? Is the Word of God their standard of behavior? If not, the light of God is not in them and they are living in the darkness of sin and error. Would you rather be guided by a blindfolded person stumbling in the dark, or by the light of the Word of God?

One of the most effective ways to keep off the casualty list is given by Paul to Timothy: "Study to show thyself approved unto God, a workman that needeth not to be ashamed, rightly dividing the word of truth" (2 Tim. 2:15). Here Paul lays out for Timothy his life's work. He must give all diligence to living a life and teaching a message of which God approves. The only way that is possible is to handle the Word of God correctly, like a bricklayer who builds his wall in strict accord with a plumb line.

For Christians the plumb line is the Bible. As we construct our lives day by day according to this standard, we will be able to discern truth from error and turn our backs on the vain babblings of the falsehood peddlers.

SPOTTING FALSE TEACHERS

Let's not deceive ourselves: False teachers abound. And the Bible makes it plain that they will have some success. Paul acknowledged this to the Ephesian elders: "For I know this, that after my departing shall grievous wolves enter in among you, not sparing the flock. Also of your own selves shall men arise, speaking perverse things, to draw away disciples after them" (Acts 20:29-30). He was the wolves on the horizon. He wasn't being a doomsayer or pessimist, but correctly interpreted the signs of the times and the words of Jesus: "Beware of false prophets, which come to you in sheep's clothing, but inwardly they are ravening wolves" (Matt. 7:15). When wolves are able to pass themselves off as sheep, the flock is in danger.

One of the best ways to spot false teachers is to listen to what they say about the sources of their messages. If they say, "Here is what God has told me," and ramble on about some dream or spectacular vision or audible voice—watch out! Place your confidence in the person who opens the Word of God and quotes it in context.

We have the admonition to "prove all things" (1 Thes. 5:21) and "try the spirits" (1 John 4:1). Jesus has given us a tool to use in proving and trying false prophets. "Ye shall know them," He says, "by their fruits" (Matt. 7:16)—not by their beguiling words or outward appearances.

Inspect the results of the questionable teacher's ministry. Are souls won to Christ? Are the people of God being grounded in Scripture? Are their lives lived for the glory of God or for personal gain and worldly ambition? And remember that false teachers come from two sources— outside the body as well as within (Acts 20:29-30). Both have a single purpose: to turn disciples away from the Lord and into the waiting arms of the devil.

Peter tells us that false teachers are unavoidable:

But there were false prophets also among the people, even as there shall be false teachers among you, who privily shall bring in damnable heresies, even denying the Lord that bought them, and bring upon themselves swift destruction. And many shall follow their pernicious ways; by reason of whom the way of truth shall be evil spoken of. And through covetousness shall they with feigned words make merchandise of you: whose judgment now of a long time lingereth not, and their damnation slumbereth not (2 Peter 2:1-3).

Their teachings are false, their ways pernicious (immoral and shameful). Their motive is covetousness, and their destiny is damnation.

It is revealing to study this passage in light of what Peter has told his readers in his previous chapter. To prepare them to withstand false teachers, he has emphasized three requirements: a heart knowledge of God and His Son, Jesus Christ; diligence in the well-rounded Christian life; and absolute confidence in the written Word of God. Have these, he seems to be saying, and false teachers will have a difficult time leading you astray.

But, he adds, these liars have appeared in days of old and will appear again. The devil never sleeps, never lets us alone. He is always on the attack. He sent false prophets to Israel and will send false teachers to the church of Christ. Unseen, like a snake in the grass, the devil places his spokesmen among the people of God to bring in his damnable heresies.

Will he succeed? Yes, many will be led astray. Not all, or even most. But when these "many" take up with the devil and follow his immoral, shameful ways, outsiders will conclude, "If that is Christianity, I want no part of it." Who can blame them? If we cannot discern the real from the counterfeit, how cay they?

Thus false teachers are a twofold danger in the spiritual war. They nullify the usefulness of those who follow them, and cause the non-Christian to turn away in disgust. And all the while the devil smiles, because his two great purposes are being achieved: He makes casualties of believers and through them throws up roadblocks to the non-Christian, keeping him from entering the gate of heaven.

THE GREAT DECEIVER

How is Satan able to get away with all this? Paul gives an answer: "I am jealous for you with a godly jealousy. I promised you to one husband, to Christ, so that I might present you as a pure virgin to Him. But I am afraid that just as Eve was deceived by the serpent's cunning, your minds may somehow be led astray from your sincere and pure devotion to Christ" (2 Cor. 11:2-3, NIV).

Eve was created to the glory of God. Yet through the subtle deception of Satan she fell, disbelieving the truth and embracing a lie. Paul's concern was that the Corinthians— infiltrated by false teachers, the agents of Satan—might similarly be deceived. Paul knew the power of Satan to create illusions. "For such are false apostles, deceitful workers, transforming themselves into the apostles of Christ" (2 Cor. 11:13-14).

Throughout the Bible we see the devil wearing various disguises, making false claims—never admitting his true identity, his true purpose, or his true nature. He is able to masquerade as an angel of light and to teach his workers to do the same. Imagine it—the ability to appear as an angel of light in order to promote a kingdom of darkness!

Paul, however, could see the truth. Just as Satan had crawled into Eden, so false teachers had crawled into Corinth. Paul uses his letter to warn the church there.

The apostle had himself received a warning from the Spirit of God: "Now the Spirit speaketh expressly, that in the latter times some shall depart from the faith, giving heed to seducing spirits, and doctrines of devils; speaking lies in hypocrisy; having their conscience seared with a hot iron; forbidding to marry, and commanding to abstain from meats, which God hath created to be received with thanksgiving of them which believe and know the truth" (1 Tim. 4:1-3). In this passage Paul does what he can to prepare Timothy to meet the challenges posed by the "doctrines of devils."

The deceivers do not seem demonic, of course. They are "seducing spirits." As Paul says, "For they that are such serve not our Lord Jesus Christ, but their own belly; and by good words and fair speeches deceive the hearts of the simple" (Rom. 16:18).

"Good words . . . fair speeches." These false teachers are usually great with words. Their speeches are quite convincing; they could sell ice makers to the Eskimos. That may tell us something about choosing a church solely on the basis of the pastor's speaking ability. A convincing speaker is not enough; he may use good words and fair speeches but not lead the people along the path of true godliness.

LEADING OURSELVES ASTRAY

There is another side to this coin. Not only false teachers get people off the track; some turn from the truth on their own.

After Jesus had laid out something of the cost of discipleship, the response of some of His followers was, "This is a hard saying; who can hear it?" (John 6:60) Many people had been attracted to Jesus and flocked around Him; some joined Him wholeheartedly, others rather loosely. When Jesus tested their allegiance, the true nature of His message began to soak in. The devoted were sifted from the casual followers who had not thought through the implications of the Lord's teaching. When they talked about a "hard saying," they meant not that it was hard to understand, but that it was hard to obey. Quite a few turned aside, as seen in John 6:66:

"From that time many of His disciples went back, and walked no more with Him." They turned aside from the life of discipleship. They had not anticipated Jesus' call to commitment, so they turned back.

People much prefer "easy sayings," as noted in 2 Timothy 4:2-3: "Preach the word; be instant in season, out of season; reprove, rebuke, exhort with all long-suffering and doctrine. For the time will come when they will not endure sound doctrine; but after their own lusts shall they heap to themselves teachers, having itching ears." Those with "itching ears" want to hear that which will "tickle their own fancies" (PH). They seek out teachers who pander to their prejudices. They shut out the truth and "wander off after man-made myths" (PH).

PRODIGALS CAN RETURN

Thank God that some wander back to the truth. One young man I know had been a fired-up Christian, but after giving heed to a false teacher he departed from the faith. His departure was along the lines of what Christ had predicted: "For there shall arise false Christs, and false prophets, and shall show great signs and wonders; insomuch that, if it were possible, they shall deceive the very elect" (Matt. 24:24).

Six years later that man reflected on his life and decided he was going nowhere in his job. He determined to go to graduate school—but didn't know what to study. Then he remembered his former life as a dedicated Christian and decided to study theology—not because he had a great desire to return to the Lord, but out of curiosity and the need to have something interesting to do.

He enrolled in a seminary which, in his words, "didn't believe anything." The school's theology was mostly cold speculation. But for one of his classes that man had to read some expositions of the Bible by Martin Luther. As he read, the Lord took hold of his life and shook him till his teeth rattled, so to speak. He recommitted his life to Christ and today is serving the Lord in a dynamic ministry.

Some shall depart—and some shall return! We rejoice in that second fact. But we also take warning: "Wherefore let him that thinketh he standeth take heed lest he fall" (1 Cor. 10:12).

BE CAREFUL WITH COUNSEL

"Blessed is the man that walketh not in the counsel of the ungodly, nor standeth in the way of sinners, nor sitteth in the seat of the scornful. But his delight is in the Law of the Lord; and in His law doth he meditate day and night. And he shall be like a tree planted by the rivers of water, that bringeth forth his fruit in his season; his leaf also shall not wither; and whatsoever he doeth shall prosper" (Ps. 1:1-3). To stay off the casualty list, we must avoid the three dangers mentioned in this verse.

First we must be very careful from whom we get counsel. The counsel of the ungodly may appear attractive, but where will it lead? How much better it is to turn to the Bible.

Second, we must not adopt the lifestyle of this sinful age. Low morals, dishonesty, cruelty, self-aggrandizement, and covetousness are the marks of the world around us, but we must adopt and live out the values of God's kingdom.

Third, we must choose our companions wisely. The devil is sly and wily. He can take the practices of the godless and make them attractive. Our best defense is God's Word.

We have a real enemy. His attacks are subtle and powerful. But they are no match for Christ. So, as the songwriter put it, "We tremble not for him." Why? Because greater is He that is in us than he that is in the world (1 John 4:4).

PART

Caught in the Crossfire

Five

NEW CHRISTIANS

He was only a baby—an abandoned baby. Staring blankly into space, too exhausted to cry, he lay motionless in a bushy nook of the jungle. Soon he would close his eyes forever. Soon he would be found and killed by the wild animals that lurked beneath the tropical trees.

But, thank God, he was discovered first by humans. A couple found the infant as they made their way through the vines and undergrowth. The woman bundled the baby in her arms and took him to their hut, where he was loved, cuddled, and fed.

But then the reality of the couple's desperate financial condition jarred them to think again. They were in a struggle to survive themselves; with their resources they couldn't keep feeding the little boy. So they tried to sell him! At first they asked $10, but no one was buying. They tried $2; still no takers. Finally, in the providence of God they met a man who ran an orphanage on a nearby island. The couple handed him the baby and walked away.

Orphanage officials named the little boy Moses, no doubt

due to his being found in the "bulrushes." But what is his future? He will grow up in a society troubled by poverty, famine, greed, hate, crime, political unrest, terrorism, and war. Will he be able to cope? It would be an understatement to say his future is uncertain.

BABES IN THE WOODS

Like little Moses, the new babe in Christ is born into a strange, uncertain world full of dangers. He is a new creation (2 Cor. 5:17). He has to learn how to survive, how to cope, how to walk with his new Lord.

He has entered a foreign land, a disconcerting experience to say the least. I learned that during my last train ride in the Netherlands. I wasn't sure of the fare or of how to know when to get off the train. The stations were not well identified either. The whole operation was obviously designed for the local people who were familiar with their surroundings.

A friend who understood the system told me, "Just watch the clocks. They are in plain view. When the clock reads 11:45, get off the train."

"But," I said, "what if the train is late?"

"It won't be. Trust me. At 11:45—get off."

So I boarded the train and watched for the clocks. I got off at 11:45, and sure enough, there was a friend to meet me. But I must confess that through it all, uncertainty was the order of the day.

No matter how old or young the new Christian is physically, no matter how much he understands about life generally, when he comes to Christ he is confronted by a different world. In a sense he has to start all over again. Unfortunately, he is born into a hostile atmosphere. The world, the flesh, and the devil set traps to thwart his progress, hinder his growth—and put him at the top of the casualty list.

THE DANGER OF FREEZING

Recently I read of a baby who froze to death. This tragedy can also happen to new Christians, spiritually speaking. In their efforts to find a church, they can meander into one that is so cold spiritually that they "freeze."

Some of us have seen people come to Christ, look for a church, and locate one near home. They don't know this church doesn't emphasize the Gospel, nor do they understand what a difference that makes. So they just settle in and try to become part of things. They attend morning worship, social activities, and bake sales to raise money for curtains in the nursery. They assume they are experiencing the norm. This may continue for ten, twenty, or thirty years.

Contrast their experience with the couple down the street who join a fired-up, Bible-teaching, Christ-centered, missions-minded church. They begin to live by the teachings of the Bible. They learn to witness and lead some of their friends and relatives to Christ. They support the Lord's worldwide mission with their gifts and prayers.

That's quite a contrast! What made the difference? The first couple walked into an icebox, and soon their little flickers of spiritual life grew so cold they were hardly noticeable. The second couple joined a warm fellowship and their flame of spirituality increased. We who know the difference in these things must do all we can to steer new Christians toward churches that will keep them warm toward the Lord.

THE DANGER OF STARVATION

Newspapers have reported tragic tales of babies who were neglected and starved to death. Such sad events have spiritual counterparts. New babes in Christ need spiritual food just as infants need milk, and there is only one food for the soul—the Bible.

Think of the danger the new believer faces in a church where the Bible is not taught. He needs to hear the Bible preached; he needs to read it, study it, and memorize it. He doesn't have to do those all at once, of course, but little by little. Without such nourishment, how can he survive, much less grow?

Because spiritual infants especially need the biblical input and fellowship a good church provides, I make a concerted effort to get them to church as soon as possible. I stress church attendance because I've never seen a believer do well over the long haul if he didn't get actively involved in the life of a local congregation. There may be exceptions, but I've never met one. Babes in Christ need a family, the warmth of a family, the warmth of fellowship with brothers and sisters in Christ.

I know *I* did. One of the greatest blessings I received as a new Christian was getting involved in a young couples' Sunday School class taught by Mrs. Karl Noorigard. She taught the Word, and my wife and I were fed. We could hardly wait for her class each week. That church was truly based on the Bible—Reverend Arlen Halverson preached it, Mrs. Noorigard taught it, and the congregation lived it! Those classes brought profound changes into every aspect of our lives. Even our refrigerator changed; no longer was it used to keep my beer cold, since I eliminated that beverage from my diet. I gave up smoking. I quit wasting Sunday afternoons at the poker table, spending them instead with our newfound friends, discussing the Word of God.

I was fascinated by these Christians. Our group included a banker, a barber, a carpenter, a mechanic, and others. They were ordinary people, yet each had a grasp of the Bible that made us want the same kind of insight and understanding. Those brothers and sisters taught us by their example how to ask God's blessing on our food. Under their influence my language took a distinct turn for the better; as an ex-Marine and railroad worker, I'd developed some salty speech patterns, and in time cursing and blasphemy were eliminated from my vocabulary. Then we met a man named Waldron Scott, who led us into Bible reading, study, and Scripture memory. We continued to be well fed.

I guess the Lord has used the memory of those early days to make me yearn to see other new Christians fed. One day someone told me, "Leroy, you are a fanatic on the subject of getting spiritual food to new Christians."

"I resent that," I replied. "I am not a fanatic on this subject. I am a *wild-eyed* fanatic!" Food is vital to the new convert as well as to the rest of us.

THE DANGER OF DISEASE

A teenager returned to America after being overseas with his missionary parents. When he filled out the school enrollment forms, he was asked whether he'd had any childhood diseases. "Oh, yes," he said. "The usual childhood diseases— malaria, dengue fever, hepatitis, amoebic dysentery, cholera, and so on."

When a person is born into the family of God, he is born into a world filled with many spiritual diseases. What a sad picture to see a new Christian who is spiritually sick! He doesn't feel like "eating" the truths of God's Word; he doesn't feel like going to work for the Lord; he doesn't feel like doing much of anything.

Just what are these spiritual diseases, and why are they so dangerous? The Apostle Peter provides insight into this when he writes, "Wherefore laying aside all malice, and all guile, and hypocrisies, and envies, and all evil speakings, as newborn babes, desire the sincere milk of the Word, that ye may grow thereby" (1 Peter 2:1-2). Here Peter lists several spiritual diseases which, if left untreated, can cause a loss of spiritual appetite and stunt the growth of the new Christian. Pretense, jealousy, and slander can cause such a spiritual "upset stomach" that there is no desire for the nutrition of the Word of God. So can other diseases such as sloth, lack of discipline, arrogance, and desire for recognition and prominence. In fact, anything that does not reflect the clear example of Jesus Christ can be considered an abnormal condition for the Christian.

Those of us who are concerned about new Christians should be prepared to help them learn how to avoid spiritual diseases—and nurse them back to health when they "catch" something. Prayer is the key to this spiritual health care; God will use the prayers of His people to see the new Christian through.

THE DANGER OF IMPROPER DIET

"Eating" the wrong things can put any Christian on the casualty list, but new believers are especially susceptible. It has already been noted that the Bible is food for spiritual growth. Likewise, sound Christian books and magazines can be used by the Spirit of God to change the new convert's pagan thought patterns and give insight and guidance in the way of Christ. The spiritual baby needs something to replace the worldly trash he may have been hooked on prior to his conversion.

When my wife and I had a ministry to cadets at the Air Force Academy, it was a delight to help wean them away from the immoral smut they had fed on and introduce them to good, solid Christian literature. A bad diet would have affected their growth. Just as two corn dogs and a coke would have made a terrible daily breakfast for those cadets, "junk" literature would have left them weak—even spoiled their appetites for quality spiritual nutrition.

It is possible to become overcautious in this area, however. Shortly after I became a Christian, I got the idea that it was wrong to read anything but the Bible. Waldron Scott sat down and straightened me out. "Would you spend an hour with men like Andrew Murray, George Muller and Charles Spurgeon?" he asked.

"Of course," I replied.

"Well, that's what their books enable you to do," he explained. "You can learn from their experiences, and in their books they can share with you what God has taught them."

Do all you can to help the new babe improve his diet. His future may depend on it.

THE DANGER OF CHILD ABUSE

In recent years our culture has been shocked by reports of child abuse. Often the abuse is inflicted by people the child knows and trusts. Spiritual child abuse is possible as well; it may come from insensitive Christians or unbelievers. I watched the effects of the latter in the life of a young man who had recently come to Christ. Some of his old drinking buddies decided to gang up on him and see if they could lead him astray. One night they came to him and began to talk about the old days. They were quite clever and persuasive; they joked around, remembering lots of "nights when. . . ." Soon the young man was in the spirit of things, and they all headed for the bar—not to do any heavy drinking, the buddies said, "Just to have a few beers for old times' sake." There would be no harm in it, they assured him.

But there was. He knew these guys, liked them, trusted them. He didn't realize they were laughing at him behind his back as they set out to lead him astray—and did. That's a form of spiritual child abuse.

THE DANGER OF PARENTAL IGNORANCE

A final peril to new believers is "parental" ignorance. We've all heard of teenage girls who give birth but haven't got a clue about being good mothers. Their babies may be mistreated, due not to evil intent but to lack of knowledge. This can happen in the spiritual realm as well. The person who leads another to Christ may have no idea how to help a new Christian "grow in grace, and in the knowledge of our Lord and Saviour Jesus Christ" (2 Peter 3:18). As a result, the new convert can suffer for lack of proper follow-up.

Fortunately, this problem has diminished in recent years. Through conferences, books, and seminars, many have become aware of their spiritual parenting responsibilities and have received instruction in the care and feeding of new Christians.

Here are four elements of follow-up which are essential in the first few weeks and months of a new Christian's spiritual life:

1. *Assurance of salvation.* Spiritual growth begins with the solid certainty of being a child of God. Do all you can to enable the new Christian to confidently express to another person his own assurance of salvation, based on his personal faith in Christ and one or more promises from the Word of God. This may require you to explain the Gospel message over and over again. It helps to share your own testimony with the new believer, showing how you came to be sure of your own salvation. Scriptures I have seen the Lord use in this regard are as follows:

And this is the record, that God hath given to us eternal life, and this life is in His Son. He that hath the Son hath life: and he that hath not the Son of God hath not life (1 John 5:11-12).

But as many as received Him, to them gave He power to become the sons of God, even to them that believe on His name: which were born, not of blood, nor of the will of the flesh, nor of the will of man, but of God (John 1:12-13).

2. *A quiet time.* Help the new convert set aside a portion of his day for Bible reading and prayer. I have found it helpful to explain why and how I conduct personal devotions. It helps to list some blessing I have received from this time with the Lord. Occasionally I have a quiet time *with* the new believer. Scriptures I regularly share at such times include these:

And in the morning, rising up a great while before day, He went out, and departed into a solitary place, and there prayed (Mark 1:35).

My voice shalt Thou hear in the morning, O Lord; in the morning will I direct my prayer unto Thee, and will look up (Ps. 5:3).

A little booklet the new convert may find helpful in this area is *Seven Minutes with God* by Bob Foster. It is available from NavPress.

3. *Preparing for setbacks and difficulties.* To be unwarned and ignorant is dangerous.

I recall the day I went to a southern California beach to try to learn body surfing. As we arrived at the beach some friends explained the basic idea to me, and I was eager to go. It was a bright, windy day; yellow flags were flying, adding to the beauty of the scene. I thought, *How nice of them to decorate the area with those pretty little yellow flags.*

I plunged into the surf, then swam out quite a ways to wait

for the big wave. When it arrived I leaped, caught the crest, and went flying toward the beach—tumbling head over heels. Terrified, I landed headfirst on the beach with my nose digging a furrow in the sand.

Next the tug of the undertow tried to drag me back under and out to sea. I fought, kicked, thrashed, and otherwise resisted the pull. Finally I crawled up the sand to safety.

Then my friends told me: Those pretty little yellow flags were there to warn beginners to beware. The surf was dangerous, the waves a bit too rugged for novices. *Now they tell me!*

But the Lord did use the incident to remind me that a little warning can prepare a new Christian for some of the dangers ahead. Scriptures I have found helpful along these lines are as follows:

There hath no temptation taken you but such as is common to man: but God is faithful, who will not suffer you to be tempted above that ye are able; but will with the temptation also make a way to escape, that ye may be able to bear it (1 Cor. 10:13).

But thanks be to God, which giveth us the victory through our Lord Jesus Christ (1 Cor. 15:57).

Fear thou not; for I am with thee: be not dismayed; for I am thy God: I will strengthen thee; yea, I will help thee; yea, I will uphold thee with the right hand of My righteousness (Isa. 41:10).

4. *Assurance of forgiveness.* The new Christian, like all of us, will fall into sin from time to time. Then what? Does he have to accept Christ all over again and be "born again" again? Of course not. He needs to apply 1 John 1:9: "If we

confess our sins, He is faithful and just to forgive us our sins, and to cleanse us from all unrighteousness."

The babe in Christ must learn that forgiveness of his sin is based on the promises of God. Some passages that may help him do so include these, in addition to 1 John 1:9:

Blessed is he whose transgression is forgiven, whose sin is covered (Ps. 32:1).

Watch ye and pray, lest ye enter into temptation. The spirit truly is ready, but the flesh is weak (Mark 14:38).

Paul's remark to the Corinthians points out another responsibility of the one who is engaged in follow-up. We must avoid behavior that might "wound" the new convert's weak conscience, causing him to stumble. To do otherwise is to sin not only against the convert but also against Christ (1 Cor. 8:12).

The life you live may well be imitated by the new believer. To him, you are a model of what the Christian life should look like. So Paul adds, "Wherefore, if meat make my brother to offend, I will eat no flesh while the world standeth, lest I make my brother to offend" (1 Cor. 8:13).

The babe in Christ faces enough problems without our adding to them by providing poor examples. We must always regulate our liberty in Christ with love for the new Christian. The spiritual infant has entered a new and unfamiliar world and needs a guide. To be a guide is a great privilege. Remember Paul's word to the Philippians: "Those things, which ye have both learned, and received, and heard, and seen in me, do: and the God of peace shall be with you" (Phil. 4:9).

If you are a new Christian, there are things you can do to keep off the casualty list. After I received Christ, I was instructed to pray that God would give me a hunger for Himself and for learning the Scriptures. It was good advice.

The devil will try to get you too busy to learn the Bible, too busy to set aside time for prayer and fellowship with other believers. If he can do this, he will have won a major victory. If you want to avoid being a casualty, do all you can to include these things in your schedule—even if it means eliminating some things you enjoy. For me it meant not hanging around the pool hall and spending so much time at the theaters. I have no idea what form this will take in your life; it may mean fewer hours in front of the television or at the country club or on the tennis or racquetball court. But let me assure you that whatever it means, it is worth it.

Must you cut out everything that's fun or relaxing? No. But you may have to modify your schedule a bit to make room for the disciplines of spiritual growth that are vital to your own survival and progress in the battle we call the Christian life.

Six

GROWING DISCIPLES

"What do you want to be when you grow up?" I was asked that question over and over when I was a youngster. First I wanted to be a cowboy, then a major league baseball pitcher, then an airplane pilot. As it turned out, I became none of those. I *did* become a disciple of Christ, a pursuit I never foresaw as a child.

How does that happen, becoming a disciple? What factors help a person toward maturity, toward becoming fruitful as a follower of Jesus? And what dangers lie along the trail of growth, waiting to put a disciple on the casualty list?

In this chapter we will look at the major hazards to growing disciples and see how a follower of Christ can stay on the "active" list. The Apostle John sets the stage:

I write unto you, little children, because your sins are forgiven you for His name's sake. I write unto you, fathers, because ye have known Him that is from the beginning. I write unto you, young men, because ye have overcome the wicked one. I write unto you, little children, because ye have known the Father. I have written unto you, fathers, because ye have known Him that is from the beginning. I have written unto you, young men, because ye are strong, and the Word of God abideth in you, and ye have overcome the wicked one (1 John 2:12-14).

In this passage, John speaks to three kinds of people:
1. *The little children in the faith.* These are the people we looked at in the last chapter, new babes in Christ.
2. *The "young men."* These Christians established a solid walk with the Lord. They have become "strong overcomers," having learned how to battle and conquer the evil one.
3. *The "fathers."* These are older disciples, those who have a deep and abiding knowledge of God. The word "father" presupposes children, so these are disciples who have worked fruitfully in the harvest, discipling others. They are men of understanding and experience.

The second group, the "young men," is the one we will consider in this chapter. Male or female, they are the ones who have placed Christ at the center of their lives; their roots are firmly fixed in the Word of God. They have established and are maintaining effective prayer lives, are in fellowship with their brothers and sisters in the church, and are reaching out with the Gospel to unsaved friends. They are fast approaching adulthood in the Christian life.

How did they get that way? When so many find themselves on the casualty list before reaching this point, how did these followers survive and flourish?

THE GOAL
To answer these questions, we must examine the disciple's goal. At what target does the new babe take aim?

The primary objective of a disciple is to become mature, dedicated, and fruitful. The Apostle Peter urged his readers to grow up—to grow in grace and in the knowledge of Christ (2 Peter 3:18). It's great for a baby to act like a baby, but it's a tragedy if that child doesn't mature.

Dedication to Christ is another sure mark of discipleship; it means the follower no longer lives for himself—is not self-centered—but is Christ-centered. Surrendering his will, he lives for the One who died for him and rose again (2 Cor. 5:15).

Fruitfulness is also included in the goal of the growing Christian. Jesus said, "Herein is My Father glorified, that ye bear much fruit; so shall ye be My disciples" (John 15:8). Fruitfulness depends on consistent fellowship with Christ; as Jesus said, "I am the Vine, ye are the branches: He that abideth in Me, and I in him, the same bringeth forth much fruit: for without Me ye can do nothing" (John 15:5).

THREE ENEMIES

Naturally there are forces which try to crowd out maturity, dedication, and fruitfulness. In' the following verse Jesus lists three of them: "And the cares of this world, and the deceitfulness of riches, and the lusts of other things entering in, choke the Word, and it becometh unfruitful" (Mark 4:19).

Here the Lord describes those whose attentions are riveted on the business of this present life. They don't just want to earn a living; they want an *abundance* of good things. They take more interest in the stock market than in the Bible. Never satisfied, they always "need" more, the latest, the most fashionable.

Their houses are stuffed with everything imaginable, and when their closets and garages and lives are packed to overflowing, they figure out how to get rid of some so they can buy other "stuff" that is "bigger" and "better."

Next the Lord speaks of "the deceitfulness of riches." The Bible teaches elsewhere that riches deceive in two ways. First, they are "uncertain" (1 Tim. 6:17) in that they "make themselves wings; they fly away as an eagle" (Prov. 23:5). They can be here today, gone tomorrow. The person who thinks wealth will make him secure can be quickly disillusioned.

Riches are also deceitful in that they don't satisfy the human heart. Recently I had dinner with one of the top men in one of America's largest corporations. He has had power, prestige, and enormous wealth—but is giving them up to devote his remaining years to helping men turn to Christ. That executive knows that Christ alone can bring real satisfaction.

Riches *do* seem worth fighting for. But "He that loveth silver shall not be satisfied with silver; nor he that loveth abundance with increase: this is also vanity" (Ecc. 5:10). Even worse, "The abundance of the rich will not suffer him to sleep" (Ecc. 5:12). Wealth does not satisfy the heart, and he who labors for it finds himself tossing and turning in bed, worrying about it.

Finally, Jesus speaks of "the lust of other things" which enter in and "choke the Word and it becomes unfruitful." What are these "other things"? They are the objects and pursuits money can buy. They may involve life in the fast lane—parties, travel, elaborate hotels, sumptuous food, and fine clothes—but they include anything which chokes out the Word of God and brings on barrenness and fruitlessness.

Every age produces its own abundance of "other things." But the result is always the same: spiritual sterility. The casualty's life becomes a howling wilderness, useless to God. Living becomes a wild goose chase for weeds, stubble, rubble—the dregs and dross of the devil's lies.

PRESCRIPTION FOR GROWTH

What can be done to prevent such a catastrophe? The Apostle Peter alludes to a solution when he says, "If these things be in you, and abound . . . ye shall neither be barren nor unfruitful. . . . For if ye do these things ye shall never fall" (2 Peter 1:8, 10). Wow! What a promise.

What are "these things" that Peter says are absolutely vital to a full and fruitful life? The following passage provides the basics:

> Simon Peter, a servant and an apostle of Jesus Christ, to them that have obtained like precious faith with us through the righteousness of God and our Saviour Jesus Christ: Grace and peace be multiplied unto you through the knowledge of God, and of Jesus our Lord, according as His divine power hath given unto us all things that pertain unto life and godliness, through the knowledge of Him that hath called us to glory and virtue: whereby are given unto us exceeding great and precious promises: that by these ye might be partakers of the divine nature, having escaped the corruption that is in the world through lust. And besides this, giving all diligence, add to your faith virtue; and to virtue knowledge; and to knowledge temperance; and to temperance patience; and to patience godliness; and to godliness brotherly kindness; and to brotherly kindness charity (2 Peter 1:1-7).

Peter begins by assuring us that growth is based on an ever-expanding knowledge of God. When our knowledge of God deepens, His grace and peace will be multiplied in our lives; "all things that pertain to life and godliness" will be ours through His divine power. What an incentive to know more of God!

How can we do that? In at least two ways:

1. *Get into the Word.* Jesus said the Scriptures teach us about Him (John 5:39). Dawson Trotman would sometimes open the Word to us and say, "Now, gang, let's enter the courtroom of the King." The Bible is the place to see the Lord.

2. *Learn through tests and trials.* When we are convinced that all things do in fact work together for good, we can face life's trials with a cheerful and thankful spirit (Col. 1:11-12). We gain knowledge of God by leaning on Him. Is it any wonder the great desire of the Apostle Paul was to "know Him"? (Phil. 3:10)

The 2 Peter 1 list continues with the "great and precious promises" of God, through which we can be "partakers of the divine nature." I find it incredible that the great Creator, God, who cannot lie, would find it necessary to put His claims to us in the form of "promises." Surely we would believe Him if He simply *said* them. Or would we? You know how it is with children; if we tell them, "I'm going to take you to the park next Saturday morning," they will feel more secure if we add, "I promise." This is the way God deals with us, putting His promises in writing. As we learn to claim these promises and build our lives on them, fruitfulness will result.

Peter did not write these things to "special" people. These promises are for all who "have obtained like precious faith with us through the righteousness of God and our Saviour Jesus Christ," who desire to grow. They are like the eager learners who "devoted themselves to the apostles' teaching" (Acts 2:42, NIV).

We must keep this fact in mind. All too often the person in the pew feels words like these are only for the clergy. Not so! We are a witnessing brotherhood; the clergy carry on their divinely appointed responsibilities of leadership, while laymen are the key to world evangelization.

The world will not be evangelized by a few pastors, but by all of us. *All* of us are to be fruitful in God's kingdom, actively reaching out to a lost world with the Gospel. The devil has deluded "average" Christians into thinking, "That's the preacher's work. That's what we pay him to do. Our job is to help him do it." There is some truth in that; each of us must help the other do his God-given job. But it works both ways, because part of the clergy's job is to "prepare God's people for works of service" (Eph. 4:11-12, NIV).

All of us are to grow in our knowledge of God and fruitfulness in His service. If we want to skip the casualty list, we must take time and trouble to keep ourselves spiritually fit by exercising ourselves in godliness (1 Tim. 4:7).

"Exercising ourselves"? Yes. Like athletes in training, we are to maintain fitness while concentrating on areas of weakness. Peter says we should do this with "all diligence." Or, as the *New International Version* has it, "Make every effort." This must not be a sideline in our lives; it should be the central thing.

EIGHT TOP PRIORITIES

At this point in the 2 Peter passage, the apostle gets specific. Drawing on his years with Christ and his knowledge of Scripture, he lists eight qualities—the cultivation of which is to take top priority in our lives:

1. *Faith.* All the other qualities have faith as their base. Jude spoke about "building up yourselves on your most holy faith" (Jude 20), also translated, "Build yourselves up on the foundation of your most holy faith" (PH). Faith is the foundation for everything else. We walk by it, not by sight (2 Cor. 5:7). It is the root of our praying. Jesus said, "And all things, whatsoever ye shall ask in prayer, believing, ye shall receive"

(Matt. 21:22). Faith enables us to believe the Gospel itself. The writer to the Hebrews spoke of those to whom the Word was ineffective because it was not "mixed with faith in them that heard it" (Heb. 4:2).

If we are to stay in the battle, our faith must be firmly grounded. Buildings with shallow foundations can crack and settle; when the foundation of a life is improperly constructed, the results can be devastating.

Not long ago I talked with a growing disciple about his concept of God's Word. His approach to the Bible was to pick and choose. He snickered at certain stories in Genesis and made light of my practice of claiming Psalms 91 and 121 when I travel. Lately I have watched this man's whole life deteriorate, and that is no coincidence. We must strive for a "rock-ribbed" faith, a faith that accepts the entire Bible as the Word of God, and its promises as true and worthy of our trust.

The growing disciple's faith must not be passive, dormant; it must be an active belief that motivates and guides. Even at its smallest, faith can bring about tremendous changes (Matt. 17:20). At its most robust it can give inner strength to withstand the worst circumstances—even when there is no visible means of support.

2. *Virtue.* The fact that Peter wants us to supplement our faith with virtue implies that it will take some effort on our part. Some people claim that any effort in any area of Christian growth smacks of "the energy of the flesh." This must be avoided, of course, but we must not let fear of it turn us into petrified Christians, ground to a halt, sitting there like bumps on a log. No, the growing disciple must take some initiative; he must open his Bible, get on his knees, and reach out to the lost.

The word for *virtue* is variously translated "goodness," "Christian energy," "moral character," "moral power," "valor," and "excellence." One facet of virtue is illustrated by a group of David's armed troops: "Of Zebulun, such as went forth to battle, expert in war, with all instruments of war, 50,000, which could keep rank: they were not of double heart" (1 Chron. 12:33). They were well trained, well equipped, disciplined, single-minded. Everything they did reflected a spirit of moral power, valor, and excellence. In the life of a growing disciple, the supreme expression of virtue is Christlikeness.

3. *Knowledge.* Ignorance of the Word is no virtue. False interpretations lead us astray. Paul spoke of those who had zeal, "but not according to knowledge" (Rom. 10:2).

When I was a student at Northwestern College, the Rev. Vance Havner visited as a chapel speaker. He told us, "I don't know which is worse—fire without the facts or facts without the fire." Both are scandals to the Christian faith. To add cold knowledge to our lives does little more than puff us up (1 Cor. 8:1); the point is to grow, not bloat. By the same token, zeal without knowledge is an embarrassment. The non-Christian laughs at it and is forced further from Christ.

The knowledge of which Peter speaks enhances our testimony, enlightens our minds, and guides our emotions. It includes the wisdom and discernment the growing disciple needs to live a Christ-centered life. Sound judgment is born of the steady and progressive acquisition of this knowledge. It has a practicality about it, and does not prompt vain speculation. It is the outgrowth of the knowledge of God that Peter spoke of in verses 2 and 3, the knowledge that sharpens our focus on Him and His will for our lives.

4. *Temperance.* This is self-restraint, control. Paul lists it a fruit of the spirit (Gal. 5:23). The self-controlled individual has an inner strength, as mentioned in Proverbs 16:32: "He that is slow to anger is better than the mighty; and he that ruleth his spirit than he that taketh a city."

The temperate Christian is not easily provoked, or seduced into following the corrupt promptings of the flesh. He has a tight reign on his inner spirit. The believer who has not mastered his inner desires will make little progress in Christian growth, because growth requires discipline.

Yet this self-control is not the legalism of Colossians 2:20-23:

> Wherefore if ye be dead with Christ from the rudiments of the world, why, as though living in the world, are ye subject to ordinances, (Touch not; taste not; handle not; which all are to perish with the using;) after the commandments and doctrines of men? Which things have indeed a show of wisdom in will worship, and humility, and neglecting of the body; not in any honor to the satisfying of the flesh.

Temperance springs from a God-given desire to please Him and walk in His way. It is meeting temptation head-on and choosing the right. To add self-control to knowledge is simply to practice what is learned—and ultimately to surrender to God's will.

5. *Patience.* This is the ability to press toward the mark in spite of hindrances, roadblocks, opposition, and persecution. It is the exact opposite of gritting your teeth and "hanging on regardless." It is steadfastness in faith.

In Scripture, patience is associated with faith in God and hope for fulfillment of His promises. It is never associated with personal bravery or heroism. It speaks of forward progress, not of just holding the fort; it runs the race (Heb. 12:1). One result of this steadfastness is a fruitful life: "But that on the good ground are they, which in an honest and good heart, having heard the Word, keep it, and bring forth fruit with patience" (Luke 8:15).

6. *Godliness.* This true devotion to God relates to our worshiping Him, both corporately and privately. It is found in our praise, adoration, and public confession of faith. At its root is a desire to be increasingly true to the Lord in thought, word, and deed. To be godly is to bring God into every aspect of our lives.

7. *Brotherly kindness.* Paul says, "Be kindly affectioned one to another with brotherly love; in honor preferring one another" (Rom. 12:10). We are told to "let brotherly love continue" (Heb. 13:1). The Thessalonians were reminded, "But as touching brotherly love ye need not that I write unto you: for ye yourselves are taught of God to love one another" (1 Thes. 4:9).

One day I was sitting in the office of the director of a large Christian ministry. In burst one of his associates, exclaiming, "You've got to do something about so-and-so. He is driving me crazy. I can't stand the guy. He rubs me the wrong way!"

Without hesitation the director replied: "You say he rubs you the wrong way. Let me ask you—does he rub your *new* nature or your *old* nature the wrong way?"

The associate looked at the floor. Finally he said, "Oh, I see," and went out the door.

It's true, isn't it? To follow the command to love the brethren takes dying to your own interests. Only Christ can enable us to be kind to the "undeserving."

8. *Love.* This supreme virtue takes in all the rest. As Paul advises, "And over all these virtues put on love, which binds them all together in perfect unity" (Col. 3:14, NIV). In Peter's list, faith is the foundation and love is the crown.

THE BOTTOM LINE

To stay off the casualty list takes diligence and desire. The growing Christian finds some clear biblical guideposts to help him remain useful; the barren, unfruitful life of which Peter warned can be avoided. The growing disciple who ends up on the scrap heap has likely taken a look at these guideposts, turned around, and run in the opposite direction.

At this point a very practical question may be forming in your mind: How do we go about attaining these virtues? Are they like the rungs of a ladder that we climb one by one?

No, I don't think they are. All these qualities are perfectly lived out by Jesus Christ, so to be like Jesus should be our primary concern. That can be done only as we watch Him, walk with Him, and submit our wills to Him. In doing this we give the Holy Spirit access to our lives to transform us into the image of Christ. It is not a matter of sheer human effort or mechanical do's and don'ts. It comes down to a life of obedient fellowship with our Lord.

As we grow in the virtues listed by Peter, we will live more productive lives. That in turn will motivate us to keep pressing on with lives that please the Lord. It won't be easy, but the Lord never said it would be. If we care about the needs of the world around us and our vital role in bringing healing and grace to that world, what else can we do?

Seven

LABORERS

I've never felt quite so worthless. Day after day I pounded the pavement, looking for work. No one was interested. "Don't call us—we'll call you," they said. I checked the want ads and called all the numbers. "Sorry, Mr. Eims," I kept hearing. I felt as if I were of no value to anybody.

Soon days became weeks. At times a ray of hope appeared but somebody else would get the job. I filled out forms for the personnel managers of large department stores and talked with owners of small businesses, but nothing happened. I became desperate, ready to take anything. But there *wasn't* anything.

For me, unemployment was hard work. The hardest part was the effect it had on my emotions; I watched morning by morning as my neighbors hopped the bus to their jobs. I would have given anything to be able to do that, but there I sat.

Unemployment in the church is also a serious matter. Unfortunately, the problem is not a lack of work. The world is full of hazards, traps, snares, and sidetracks that cause the

Lord's laborers to stop laboring. And many don't bother even to enter the work force in the first place.

A CHURCH JOB SHORTAGE?

One day I asked a friend of mine who pastors a fairly large church, "How many members are there in your church?"

"Close to 5,000," he answered.

"Let me ask you another question," I said. "How many people are *involved?* I mean, how many people sing in the choir, work in the Sunday School or as ushers or Bible Study leaders, serve on boards or committees, volunteer to work with children or youth—*everything?*

"Oh," he answered, "a good estimate would be around 1,500 people." I made a mental note. That left 3,500 people with nothing to do, unemployed.

On another occasion I asked another pastor friend how many members were in his church. "Around 800," he replied.

"How many of those have jobs in the church?" I asked.

"Well," he said, "I've never thought about it, but I'd guess there would be around 300."

I made another mental note. There were 500 people in that church with nothing to do! The jobs were all taken; the boards were full, the choir packed, the Bible studies led. Perhaps there was a stray job here or there, and of course some people were filling more than one position. But hundreds of people were just sitting there with nothing to do— nothing, that is, if church work is all there is to the Lord's work.

There are two ways to work for the Lord, however. There is *church work,* and there is *the work of the church.* It is in the latter field that the average man and woman in the pew should shine. If each of those 5,000 or 800 "unemployed" church members saw himself as a person called and commissioned by Christ to carry the Gospel into the world, there would be more than enough work for everyone. If the objective of every Christian was to become a spiritually qualified laborer, we would all be up to our necks in work!

WHEN LABORERS BECOME CASUALTIES

Those who never go to work for Christ are already on the casualty list. But what about growing disciples who become well-equipped, spiritually qualified laborers? All too often, even as they are reaching the lost and helping people grow, tragedy occurs. They quit laboring, walk off the job, hand in their resignations. The tragedy is doubled because laborers are so few and the harvest is so great.

Why does this happen? What causes people to "give notice" and leave the harvest field? Several reasons follow.

CROP FAILURE

Sometimes a worker toils long and hard but sees no fruit. A prolonged "dry spell" leaves him discouraged. He has seemed to do everything right, but to no avail. He has witnessed consistently, but no one has come to Christ; after praying for and working with the new Christian, he sees no progress. Finally, out of sheer desperation and despair, he simply quits.

I must confess I don't know why such dry spells occur. Perhaps God wants at times to do more *in* us than *through* us. He could be testing our faith. Whatever the cause, unfruitfulness can cause the disheartened laborer to leave the field.

Even when a worker has had a generally fruitful life, there come times when the ministry seems to dry up. This, of course, is no new problem. Remember the testimony of Habakkuk: "Although the fig tree shall not blossom, neither shall fruit be in the vines; the labor of the olive shall fail, and the fields shall yield no meat; the flock shall be cut off from the fold, and there shall be no herd in the stalls: yet I will rejoice in the Lord, I will joy in the God of my salvation" (Hab. 3:17-18).

At one point in his life, Habakkuk looked out on the fields and they were barren. The fig tree, a prime source of food, was withered; the olive tree was not producing; acres which should have been lush with waving grain were like deserts; even the cattle were dying. But he continued to place his hope in God and to rejoice in spite of adversity. That is no easy task. But when the laborer surrenders his own ideas of success and finds God as his true source of joy and satisfaction, he can continue to enter the field with an expectant heart. Crop failure need not drive the worker from the field.

FATIGUE

Weariness is a major problem that affects many. Strangely enough, however, much fatigue is self-caused. The laborer is often a highly motivated individual; he sees his work as important, and sees himself as a vital factor in it. So he tackles the job with vigor and enthusiasm, but doesn't know how to pace himself. Because his work is so important, he doesn't want to "pamper" himself with time-outs, days off, or vacations. So he goes and goes, and has a difficult time admitting that he needs to slow down.

But even Jesus got tired and sat down to rest awhile: "Jesus therefore, being wearied with His journey, sat thus on the well" (John 4:6). At one point in His training of the Twelve, Jesus prescribed a break in the schedule. "And He said unto them, 'Come ye yourselves apart into a desert place, and rest a while:' for there were many coming and going, and they had no leisure so much as to eat" (Mark 6:31).

I once heard a preacher say that unless we occasionally come apart, we *will* come apart. Jesus, as the leader of this band of laborers in training, knew this and saw the need to pace activities. Apparently the lesson was not lost on these men; though they were highly motivated people involved in the greatest work on earth, we do not read of any of them leaving the field due to fatigue.

"NOBODY CARES"

Let's say some laborers in a local church are giving themselves wholeheartedly to witnessing and following up. They are having moderate success. Each of these men and women has led at least one person to Christ. Each is excited. Yet whenever the pastor gives a commendation from the pulpit, these workers are never mentioned. The choir receives well-earned praise; the ushers are thanked publicly; there is a day set aside to honor Sunday School workers. But this "unofficial" laboring force is ignored.

These workers are not evangelizing in order to be seen and praised by men, but like the rest of us they need a pat on the back now and then. As the weeks and months wear on, though, they continue to labor unappreciated. On baptism Sundays one or more of their converts appear before the church, but the evangelists are unnoticed.

Eventually one or more of these workers grows discouraged. *Why are we doing all this if no one really cares?* they ask themselves. In time some drop out and get into a ministry in the church which seems to be more welcome and commended.

For any laborers who identify with this problem, Paul's advice is apt: "And whatsoever ye do, do it heartily, as to the

Lord, and not unto men; knowing that of the Lord ye shall receive the reward of the inheritance: for ye serve the Lord Christ" (Col. 3:23-24). Keep it up! If you're winning souls to Christ, I'm sure it pleases Him.

OFF-CENTERED LIFE

Like every believer, the laborer is to live a Christ-centered life. This should be easily understood by the growing disciple; most of the training he receives points in that direction. He is urged to get his roots down into Christ (Col. 2:6-7). The focus of his discipling is to help establish a deep and abiding fellowship with Christ in new converts. But when he enters the labor force, he can be subtly led away from being Christ-centered to being ministry-centered. After all, the command is there to perform ministry—to preach the Gospel to one and all (Mark 16:15) and make disciples of all nations (Matt. 28:18-20).

To do the Lord's work today takes thought, creativity, energy, new approaches, prayer, and dedication. With all that to preoccupy us, we can see how easy it would be for our focus to shift from Christ Himself to Christ's work. But that change of focus contains the seeds of disaster. The ministry must not be our master; Christ is our Master. As He pointed out, no one can serve two lords (Matt. 6:24). Christ, by the Holy Spirit, can comfort and encourage our hearts—but the ministry, if it dominates our lives, can run us ragged.

The Apostle Paul pointed out that Christ is our life (Col. 3:4). He told the church at Philippi, "For to me to live is Christ, and to die is gain" (Phil. 1:21). No one took laboring more seriously than Paul, who said, "I will very gladly spend and be spent for you" (2 Cor. 12:15). But he was not consumed by his work. His love and dedication were for Christ, not a ministry plan. So it must be with us if we are to avoid the casualty list and "finish our course" as he did. As Dawson Trotman often said, "Never get so involved in the work of the kingdom that you don't have time for the King. "

Not long ago we installed a new pastor in our church. A friend of his who had been in the ministry for about two years spoke at the installation service. He told of his hectic schedule and the mountain of work that faced him each day. "If there is anything I've learned, it is this: Spend time with God," the pastor said. That's the way to prevent off-centeredness.

Early in my work as a Navigator representative, I learned the value of spending mornings with God, afternoons with guys I was helping in the faith, and evenings split between my family and ministry. Most evenings I spent at home, but some I spent at evangelistic activities. I found that it is difficult to strike the proper balance between fellowship with Christ and the work of Christ, but it is absolutely vital to do it. If we don't, our lives get off center and can fly apart.

LACK OF PREPARATION

No pursuit is more important than getting the Gospel to every person. For that reason some laborers are sent to the field before they are ready. An equipper may see the vast, overripe harvest and be burdened to do all he can to help. He is working with two or three growing disciples for whom he has high hopes; one especially seems to be doing remarkably well. So the equipper changes the focus of the convert's training, gives him some help in becoming a laborer, and turns him loose.

But it's too soon. The laborer plunges into the work, only to discover that he is in over his head. There are problems for which he has no answers, situations he is unprepared to meet. He is not equipped to handle the pressures, the complexities, the demands that come his way.

If the equipper is on the ball, he will see his error and do what he can to extricate the worker and prepare him further. But if the laborer doesn't get the help he needs, the devil can use the mess to discourage him, make him feel like a failure, and eventually cause him to drop out of the ministry and onto the casualty list. The church's task is huge and urgent, but his is all the more reason to make certain that when a worker heads for the harvest, he is there for a lifetime.

There are no guaranteed training plans, of course. And there will always be problems and pressures that bring us closer to the Lord, where we cry out for strength and wisdom. Even the Apostle Paul was "perplexed" (2 Cor. 4:8); there were times when he saw no way out of certain dilemmas. But it was not because he was in the field too soon. Let the equipper not be in such a hurry that the fields are full of inexperienced and untrained laborers. The demands of the harvest tax even the "old hands."

GREENER GRASS

The laborer is subtly tempted to leave his field for something "better." He may grow weary of involvement with the un-saved; after all, some non-Christians are a real mess, and it takes grace and patience to be around them. Some are fun and a challenge, but after months or years of putting up with dirty jokes, cigarette smoke, foul language, and blasphemy, the laborer may long for a return to an easier life. Equipping new Christians can also be a vexation. The worker answers the same questions year after year, faces the same struggles to get converts on their feet and living for the Lord.

One morning the laborer may wake up and decide he has had enough. *There are lots of easier ways of serving the Lord,* he thinks. So he packs up and leaves the work force.

The laborer needs periodic reminders of the key role he plays in doing God's work. Otherwise his vision can become blurred; he can lose perspective. The needs of the world are so great that we cannot afford to lose one laborer to the casualty list. Workers are too valuable, both to the Lord of the harvest and to the people who need the ministry.

COLDNESS

Sometimes ministry becomes a burden, the Bible becomes dry, and prayer becomes a duty. When that happens, the laborer does well to take time to get thawed out and fired up again. A day alone with the Lord can do wonders to clear the vision, warm the heart, and fire the spirit.

I have found great benefit in arranging for a day off by myself where there are no telephones, no people, and no activities to tug at my coat sleeve. I take my Bible, a writing pad, a hymnal, and a devotional book or biography of a man or woman of God. I like to begin by going through a hymn or two, then spend time in prayer. Next I read the Bible—unhurriedly. Then I pray some more and read a chapter or two in my devotional book or biography. The purpose is to give the Holy Spirit an opportunity to speak to me. As insights come, I make notes and pray over them. The process doesn't take forever; a day will usually suffice.

Another valuable help along this line is to set aside time for a periodic discipleship or disciple-making conference. The messages and fellowship can help prevent laborer's burnout; new ideas surface and new vigor results.

STICKING WITH IT: THE REWARDS

With so many traps set for the worker, is it worth it to persevere? I know from experience that it is. My wife and I once ministered to cadets at the Air Force Academy in Colorado Springs. It was a challenge, especially because many restrictions were imposed on civilians in their contact with cadets. The men themselves were also limited as to when they could leave the Academy and go into town.

As I prayed for ideas on how to reach these men, the Lord brought a plan to mind. Soon our family moved to a large home near the Academy; we called it our "soul trap." We invited the cadets there for food and relaxation. My wife worked behind the scenes practicing hospitality, cooking tons of food which the guys ate with gusto. A man in New Mexico bought a Ping-Pong table and other games for us to use in our basement. Soon our soul trap was in full swing.

Today some of the men who were reached in that home are serving Christ on five continents. Two people—my wife and the man from New Mexico—served those men behind the scenes by practicing hospitality and generosity. As these men came to Christ, they would tell how others—parents, Sunday School teachers, pastors, church bus drivers—had also been used by the Lord to eventually bring them to Himself. Each of those workers was needed and important.

All of us should take heart as we fulfill the responsibilities God has given us, whether we are ushers or evangelists or cooks. In the words of Paul, "Let us not be weary in well doing: for in due season we shall reap, if we faint not" (Gal. 6:9).

Eight

LEADERS

When you first enter the canyon, it's not so bad. The walls are far apart. But when you've hiked up the trail for fifteen or twenty minutes the walls sort of close in on you; the trail narrows and the walls tower to the sky.

Then you see them: huge rocks sitting atop the canyon walls. *What if they broke loose?* you wonder. Nothing would be safe in their path. They would uproot trees and smash bushes and wildflowers. Wildlife would be endangered; bighorn sheep, deer, and the occasional bear would be crushed by the granite monoliths.

And you, of course, would be in imminent peril. As you stand there you can see where smaller rocks have broken loose with little result. But those big ones way up on top—if they started down, there would be all kinds of trouble.

That's how it is with "higher-ups" in the church. The higher a church leader goes and the bigger his responsibilities become, the greater the damage he can do if he takes a spiritual tumble. You've heard of these tragedies; a preacher runs off with a pianist, a Christian leader leaves his wife and kids, a missionary is sent home from the field because of some personal problem, the parachurch executive turns to an occupation that promises an easier life, and on and on. Why? What happened to these people? There they were, like huge chunks of granite, and all of a sudden they came crashing down.

In this chapter we will look at some of the things the devil has used to bring down the "high and mighty"—and I use that term in the complimentary sense. Many of these leaders had huge responsibilities and carried them well. Unfortunately, when one of these top leaders falls, scores or hundreds or even thousands of people are hurt.

PRESSURES AT THE TOP

Here are some of the factors that cause leaders to give up their roles in the spiritual war:

1. *Ambition.* When I was a student at the University of Washington in Seattle, Senator Robert Taft came to our campus to lecture. After he finished, a few of us gathered around him to ask questions. The next day a picture of the event appeared in the student newspaper, and there I was standing right next to the senator! I carried that picture in my notebook for weeks and showed it to lots of people. I'd had my picture taken with a U.S. senator; I was *somebody!*

That incident was a rather harmless part of my growing-up years. But when a Christian leader is possessed by the desire to "be somebody," it can do great harm. Jesus Himself, who "was in all points tempted like as we are, yet without sin" (Heb. 4:15), was tempted in the wilderness concerning this very thing. Imagine! He was offered "All the kingdoms of the world, and the glory of them." (Matt. 4:8). But the temptation failed because in the heart of Jesus was no ambition, no desire for grandeur, authority, or power. The Apostle Paul also shrugged off every notion of personal ambition and self-glory (1 Thes. 2:6).

This does not mean that attempting great things for God is categorically sinful. To dream great dreams and desire to be used of God is perfectly all right. One's motive is the key; the glory of God must be central to our desires and prayers. But unsanctified ambition can dislodge the leader and send him crashing down the canyon wall. Remember Jesus' warning regarding the motive of the hypocrites, "that they may have glory of men" (Matt. 6:2).

DESIRE FOR POPULARITY

Pastor X *has* "become somebody." He attracts a worldwide television audience; his voice is heard on radios around the globe; his books have sold in the millions. People come from miles around when he shows up to preach. His own church is attended by thousands; all three Sunday morning services are packed out, and hundreds jam into the overflow room to watch and listen on closed circuit TV. All this is fine—unless Pastor X begins to believe he deserves all that adulation.

Popularity is a danger not only for well-known leaders. It can overtake the country preacher too. Every week after the sermon each church member files past and tells Pastor Y what a great preacher he is. He may well be, but all that popularity can go to his head and be his downfall. Remember, the God of the universe says, "Even every one that is called by My name: for I have created him for My glory, I have formed him; yea, I have made him" (Isa. 43:7). It's hard to remain little in your own eyes when everyone else is telling you how great you are. Popularity can come from the elevating hand of God, but can also result in destruction if the leader misinterprets his success.

SELF-PITY

Pastor Z wanted to lead a large church he'd had his eye on. But someone else was selected. Then the plan he'd proposed and pushed through the church committees turned out to be a flop—through no fault of his own—and he got the blame. Then he started feeling sorry for himself. Finally he quit.

Leaders can find themselves indulging in self-pity or being angry at an organization, church, or individual when their expectations aren't met. The best antidote is a healthy dose of the sovereignty of God—believing that all things do in fact work together for good to those who love Him.

I know victory in this area is possible, because I've observed it firsthand. A large church was looking for a youth director, and a volunteer worker in the youth department was asked by the Christian education director to submit his application. After prayer and counsel the young man did so—along with over sixty others from across the country.

The choice boiled down to two—this young man and one other. Both really wanted the job. My young friend began to dream about what he would do if selected—changes he would make, the direction he would head. Finally the verdict was announced: The other person got the job.

What did the young man do? Instead of pitying himself, he threw his wholehearted support behind the new leader. He began to pray for the leader and continued his own involvement as a volunteer worker. He accepted the whole thing as the leading of God and pressed ahead with great joy and enthusiasm. And in recent months God has unexpectedly opened up something far better for him—an opportunity for service that is exciting and has unlimited worldwide potential. Things have truly worked out to the glory of God because that young man did not allow himself the luxury of self-pity.

SHORTSIGHTEDNESS

A leader must be a man or woman of vision, one who sees more clearly and further into the future than others. If he doesn't, he doesn't lead. He must be able to spot opportunities and turn them into realities.

I read recently of such a man in *The Wall Street Journal.* The article told of Eli Tisona, who was sitting in his home in Israel when he saw a TV news clip about Jamaica. The scenes of lush green foliage gave him an idea.

Within days he had someone heading for Jamaica to bring back samples of Jamaican water and soil for testing. Soon a partnership was formed with the Jamaican government; the Israelis leased 4,500 acres of fertile farm land to grow vegetables, bananas, and ornamental flowers and nursery shrubs. The Israelis also scattered ponds around the site, where they expect to raise more fish per year than are harvested in all of Israel.

How did it all start? With a man who was sitting at home, watching a TV news story about a land thousands of miles away. Most of us would have seen nothing special, but this man looked at those lush, rolling hills and saw a vision of what could be.

"Where there is no vision, the people perish" (Prov. 29:18). Christian leaders need God's help to see the jobs that need doing. Otherwise people have no focus for their energies; they go off in various directions, unrestrained.

Years ago I saw a cartoon that deeply affected my life. It pictured two cavemen. One was saying, "Unfortunately, all the important discoveries have already been made." Too many leaders have the mindset of that caveman. In the midst of a sin-sick world that cries out for help, they sit content. Lack of vision may not cause leaders to lose their organizational positions, but can make them so ineffective as to be practically useless to God.

INFLEXIBLE SUPERVISORS

Another problem that often plagues the young leader is being forced to function within a supervisor's hidebound, worn-out, traditional approaches. Restricted by outmoded rules and regulations, the leader is unable to flex his muscles and venture in new directions. He gets no encouragement when he makes a new discovery; he is told to quiet down, not to rock the boat.

I saw this principle at work at a rest stop on an interstate highway. A young boy was studying the map on the wall with great interest and intensity. Suddenly he made what for him was a marvelous discovery: The map told him right where he was! By following the road signs, he could see where he was going. Excited by his discovery, he went up to his mother and tried to get her to look at the map. "Look! Look!" he said. "We're right here. We've only got five more bridges [he meant interchanges] to go and we'll be at Grandmother's road."

His mother looked at him and shouted, "Shut up and get in the car."

"But look," he pleaded, "we've got only five more bridges to go and we'll be at Grandmother's road."

"I told you to get in the car," his mother snarled. With that the lad did as he was told, a look of disappointment clouding his face.

I was saddened by the scene. What a great opportunity to commend and encourage the lad! He had figured things out by himself. But his spirit was crushed by his mother's lack of interest.

I have watched this happen in the lives of young leaders. They make a discovery, find a new approach, improve on some practice. But no one will listen. Frustration clouds their spirits. Sometimes they give up in disgust and walk away— and a powerful force for good is lost to the kingdom of God.

Barnabas was a "son of encouragement" (Acts 4:36, NIV). Supervisors of young leaders especially need that spirit of encouragement to keep the young leader fired up and on track. It doesn't cost much to be an encourager, and the dividends are great. If the young leader is never encouraged nor allowed to experiment, he can end up on the spiritual casualty list.

LUST

Lust has proven to be a deadly enemy of leaders. Temptation can strike at home or away; a pastor may find himself alone with a distraught, weeping woman who needs comfort, while a speaker can find himself in a strange city, feeling lonely and wanting companionship.

I know one young leader who was on a preaching tour in Germany. He was alone in his hotel room when a knock came at his door. A maid wanted to come in and fix the curtain, so he let her in and sat down. She clambered onto the bed and reached high above her head to repair the damaged curtain rod. He glanced up at her just as she looked down at him and smiled.

The man leaped to his feet, bolted out the door, and went to the restaurant for a cup of coffee and toast. He was neither hungry nor thirsty, but knew his room was no place for him at that moment. He was following Paul's advice to Timothy: "flee ... youthful lusts" (2 Tim. 2:22).

But make no mistake: This sin is not the private domain of the young leader. Scripture states, "For she hath cast down many wounded: yea, many *strong* men have been slain by her" (Prov. 7:26, italics added). Lust has produced casualties in every "division" of the Lord's army.

For five years an overseas missionary trained a young national for the ministry. The young man showed great promise; he was steady in his growth and walk with the Lord; he displayed many God-given gifts that especially suited him for effective evangelism and discipleship. The missionary had high hopes that this young leader-in-training would one day be a powerful force for God in that part of the world. But then the young man became involved with a non-Christian girl, and at last report was in danger of ending up on the spiritual scrap heap.

That man joins thousands of others who have fallen into this sin through the years. Remember the words of Nehemiah: "Did not Solomon king of Israel sin by these things? Yet among many nations was there no king like him, who was beloved of his God, and God made him king over all Israel: nevertheless even him did outlandish women cause to sin" (Neh. 13:26).

FAILING FAITH

Another snare for leaders is mentioned in this promise of Jesus to Peter: "I have prayed for thee that thy faith fail not" (Luke 22:32). If a leader's faith fails, his own life is devastated—and those involved with him are hurt in many ways.

Failing faith destroys all sense of perspective; without that, one cannot lead. When I was in high school, a classmate and I took the front seat out of his car, bored some holes in the floorboard, crouched on the floor, and drove down to the highway. Drivers of oncoming cars saw what they supposed to be a car with no driver; we managed to stay on our side of the road by watching the center line through the holes we had bored. This fun but dangerous stunt illustrates what it's like to try to lead a ministry when you have no perspective due to failing faith. You have only a sense of where you are at the moment—no idea of where you're going or what's ahead.

Failing faith also prompts a false sense of values. Molehills become mountains; things of great value appear worthless. There is the temptation to give up.

Robust faith, on the other hand, promotes a correct perspective and sense of values. When Billy Graham preached at Dawson Trotman's funeral service, he said, "To Daws, God was big and the world was small." For that reason the founder of the Navigators could work for the evangelization of the world with enthusiasm and confidence. The job was small in comparison to the greatness of God. But when faith fails, the task can overwhelm the leader.

The list of things the devil may use to bring down the Christian leader is probably endless. My friend Warren Myers "prays defensively" against many of them: lust, wrong involvement with the opposite sex, covetousness, possession-centeredness, pride, a critical spirit and tongue, wrong doctrine, and spiritual coldness. He says his wife Ruth includes many of these in her defensive praying, and adds anxiety, self-reliance, and fear of disapproval. To this I would add unfaithfulness in the basics, loss of zeal in witness, ministering the Word in the energy of the flesh as opposed to the power and fullness of the Holy Spirit, and becoming weary in well-doing.

It is obvious that the leader faces many foes in his work. Thank the Lord for such promises as 1 Corinthians 15:57: "But thanks be to God, which giveth us the victory through our Lord Jesus Christ."

STAYING ON TOP

In addition to praying defensively, there are at least six things the leader must do to prevent winding up on the casualty list:

1. *Provide an example.* The leader must embody the

virtues to which the congregation aspires. The Apostle Peter admonished elders to avoid "being lords over God's heritage" but to be "examples to the flock" (1 Peter 5:3).

2. *Minister as a servant.* Jesus said the leader must see himself as the servant of all (Matt. 20:25-28). The Apostle Paul told the Corinthians he would "very gladly spend and be spent" for them (2 Cor. 12:15). He reminded the church at Thessalonica that he was "delighted to share with you not only the Gospel of God but our lives as well" (1 Thes. 2:8, NIV).

3. *Work wholeheartedly.* If a leader does not really have his heart in the game, his people will soon lose heart as well. If a basketball coach continually displays an "I don't care if we win or lose" attitude, players won't care either. The Apostle Paul challenged the Romans to be "fervent in spirit" in serving the Lord (Rom. 12:11). Earlier he had told them, "I am . . . eager to preach the Gospel" (Rom. 1:15, NIV). The spirit of an eager, fired-up leader rubs off on followers.

4. *Pray for the people.* Epaphras, the founder and leader of the church at Colossae, is a tremendous challenge in this regard. He had gone from Colossae to Rome to talk to the Apostle Paul. What did he do in the big city? Go sightseeing? Buy postcards? No; Paul says, "Epaphras, who is one of you, a servant of Christ, saluteth you, always laboring fervently for you in prayers, that ye may stand perfect and complete in all the will of God" (Col. 4:12). Epaphras was a caring leader, a concerned leader—a good leader. He diligently prayed for the people.

5. *Teach the Word.* The Apostles saw thousands of people come to Christ, yet continued to feel a great burden to teach new converts. This is evident by Luke's comment: "And daily in the temple, and in every house, they ceased not to teach and preach Jesus Christ" (Acts 5:42).

6. *Guide the ministry.* Leaders are to be overseers

(1 Peter 5:2). This involves getting a clear mental picture of where the ministry is heading, how it should be carried out, and communicating this to people. Much of the leader's insight will come as he listens to his close advisers; guidance comes from the bottom up as well as from the top down.

HELPING YOUR LEADERS

But all this is to no avail if the people are not with the leader in spirit. The leader cannot do a good job if his followers aren't doing all they can to make things work. Here are a few tips for followers who want to help their leaders:

1. *Pray for them.* Just as leaders must pray for the people, so the people must pray for them. Paul constantly encouraged this. He told the Colossians to "pray for us" (Col. 4:3, NIV). He wrote to the Romans, "I urge you, brothers, by our Lord Jesus Christ and by the love of the Spirit, to join me in my struggle by praying to God for me (Rom. 15:30, NIV).

2. *Pitch in.* Help carry the load. Be available when leaders need you. Remember the words of Jesus, "And if ye have not been faithful in that which is another man's, who shall give you that which is your own?" (Luke 16:12)

3. *Support them financially.* Give cheerfully. This was the commendation of the Lord Jesus for a woman who came into the house of Simon the leper and annointed Jesus with oil: "She hath done what she could" (Mark 14:8). That's all the Lord asks of us—to give as we are able.

4. *Be an encourager.* It must have been tremendous for the apostles to have Barnabas, the "son of encouragement," on the team. The devil can use many things to discourage your leaders. Be there with a pat on the back and a word of cheer.

5. *Include leaders and their families in your social life.* All too often Christian leaders are isolated from the lives of

"regular" people who consider them to be "men of the cloth." Jesus was invited to the wedding in Cana of Galilee; He was not shut out because of His special calling and place in God's kingdom. It means a lot to leaders to be able to count people as their friends (John 15:15).

6. *Do what you can to help leaders' kids stay on the "straight and narrow."* Love them. Include them on days at the beach, the mountains, the amusement park, the game. Have fun with them; help disciple them. All too often Christian leaders' kids feel that because their dads don't play professional football or drive eighteen-wheelers they have to prove to their friends that they aren't sissies. Help leaders' kids feel accepted and cared for. Do what you can do to enable them to increase in wisdom and stature and in favor with God and man (Luke 2:52). In so doing, you may help a leader *and* a child steer clear of the casualty list.

PART

A Winning Strategy

Nine

DEVOTION

So far we've considered the snares, difficulties, problems, and pressures which can put Christians on the casualty list. Now we'll look in detail at the principles outlined in God's Word which can help keep us on the "active" list in the spiritual war.

SURRENDER: THE BEGINNING AND END
The "bottom line" of the Christian life is surrender to the lordship of Christ. Without this, all else is futile. We can speak of our love for the Word of God, our dedication to prayer, our desire to obey God's statutes—but so did the Pharisees, and they were soundly rebuked by our Lord. Surrender is a daily need. Every day options present themselves to us—options that boil down to choosing self or the Saviour.

Consider the fact of Christ's lordship:

Let this mind be in you, which was also in Christ Jesus:

who, being in the form of God, thought it not robbery to be equal with God: but made Himself of no reputation, and took upon Him the form of a servant, and was made in the likeness of men: and being found in fashion as a man, He humbled Himself, and became obedient unto death, even the death of the cross. Wherefore God also hath highly exalted Him, and given Him a name which is above every name: that at the name of Jesus every knee should bow, of things in heaven, and things in earth, and things under the earth; and that every tongue should confess that Jesus Christ is Lord, to the glory of God the Father (Phil. 2:5-11).

Surrender to Christ's reign as Lord in our lives begins with humility, a lowly mindset, and death to self. Christ is our perfect example of these; He left heaven, came to earth, suffered, and died on a cross. Why? He had every "right" to remain in heaven, His "rightful" home. He was the eternal God. But He "lowered" Himself, "emptied" Himself. He didn't cling to His "rights." He did not count equality with God a thing to be "rightfully" clung to but surrendered it all.

The eternal Christ became Jesus, "Mary's boy child," who would save His people from their sins. If the thought staggers us, it is with good reason. The incarnation is a mystery.

But there is another event in Christ's life that is also filled with mystery. It took place in the Garden of Gethsemane when Jesus prayed, "Father, if Thou be willing, remove this cup from Me: nevertheless not My will, but Thine, be done" (Luke 22:42). Just as Christ emptied Himself to become a baby, so in Gethsemane He emptied Himself of His own will, gave up His "rights" as God's beloved Son, and surrendered Himself to the will of the Father.

There is a very important point here that must not be missed. Christ did more than take upon Himself the likeness of a man; He took upon Himself the "form of a servant." If He had come to earth as the Apostles saw Him on the Mount of Transfiguration, His redemptive surrender, suffering, and death would not have been accomplished.

The application of all this to you and me is clear; just as the Lord "humbled Himself, and became obedient unto death," so must we. If you and I would stay off the casualty list and serve the Lord all our days, we must deeply surrender to His lordship. Just as He did not cling to His "rights," neither can we.

But when we surrender, are we in for lives of unfulfillment? Did Christ regret His decision to go to Bethlehem, Gethsemane, or Golgotha? No. Isaiah tells us, "He shall see of the travail of His soul, and shall be satisfied" (Isa. 53:11). Likewise, if we receive any true satisfaction in this life, it will come as we surrender to Christ's lordship and do His will.

THE SENSIBLE SURRENDER

Surrendering to Christ is the most sensible thing we can do. To trade the temporal for the eternal is not a foolish act; to build a house on rock instead of sand is quite reasonable. Consider the words of the apostle: "The world and its desires pass but the man who does the will of God lives forever" (1 John 2:17, NIV).

Two verses previously, John has warned us not to love the world. Why? Because our hearts cling to the things we love. We delight in them, think of them, dream about them. Like the stench of burning garbage permeates the atmosphere, so the world can saturate our souls.

When our thoughts and dreams are filled with this world, we become worldly—and that is deadly. Why? Because our lives are captured by that which is passing away. It is the nature of this world to be temporal, to pass from the scene.

Its beauty is fading, its foundations crumbling. On the surface it all looks so solid, so attractive, so real—but its days are numbered.

Would you deposit your money in a bank that you knew was about to go bust? Would you buy a condominium on the fourteenth floor if you knew the foundation of the whole building was about to collapse? Would you agree to drive in a stock car race if you knew all four of your vehicle's tires were about to blow? Would you board a plane if you knew the flight crew was dead drunk, the plane was nearly out of fuel, and the landing gears were going to fail? Would you build a home on the rim of an active volcano?

If you answered no to those questions, why would you want to put your future in the world's hands? It is right now passing away, sliding steadily toward the precipice of doom, rusting out from under us. With a swift and sure contrast, John tells us that the one who has surrendered to the will of Christ "lives forever." So surrendering to Him is very sensible indeed.

THE LIVING SURRENDER

Paul says, "I beseech you therefore, brethren, by the mercies of God, that ye present your bodies a living sacrifice, holy, acceptable unto God, which is your reasonable service. And be not conformed to this world: but be ye transformed by the renewing of your mind, that ye may prove what is that good, and acceptable, and perfect, will of God" (Rom. 12:1-2). It is only through surrendering to Christ that we can discover a life that is good, acceptable, and perfect.

Paul's sacrificial imagery in this passage is from the Old Testament. He reminds us of Jewish believers who presented their sacrifices to the Lord, giving something from their possessions—something outside themselves. But here he asks New Testament believers to cast themselves on the "altar" as living sacrifices to do God's will. He calls on us to do this in response to God's pardon and sure promise of eternal life; the reasonable response is give our bodies and souls to the service of God.

The Old Testament sacrifice was consumed on the altar in a few minutes; our sacrifices are to last a lifetime. But it will not be a life of gloom and drudgery. It will be good, acceptable and perfect—and it's hard to improve on that.

THE STEP OF SURRENDER

The step of surrender must be made by faith. Only *after* my surrender to the lordship of Christ can I discover His will. I can't bargain with God, saying, "Lord, let me test it out. Let me try it for a while, and then if I like that sort of life I'll make the surrender." God's good, acceptable, perfect will is revealed to those who trust Him and take the step.

Jesus was getting at this principle when He said, "If any man will do His will, he shall know of the doctrine, whether it be of God, or whether I speak of Myself' (John 7:17). First you do, *then* you know. When you set your human will free to do the will of God, it is then and only then that God opens up the life He describes as good, acceptable, and perfect.

When the shackles of self are removed, God's power fills your life and sets you free to soar in the sky of His great and eternal purposes. What an astounding idea! One would think that only a few privileged wise men and women would ever be able to discover the life God Almighty describes as the best. But no—it is for the likes of you and me! Still it requires a living sacrifice—a sacrifice of the life lived under His lordship.

There's no reason to dread such a sacrifice. It's a step we can make with eager anticipation. Isaiah's words apply:

"Remember ye not the former things, neither consider the things of old. Behold, I will do a new thing; now it shall spring forth; shall ye not know it? I will even make a way in the wilderness, and rivers in the desert" (Isa. 43:-18-19).

Those words were spoken when God's people had lost heart. Their captivity had been hard. God was assuring them of their release; He would break the power of their captors. Realizing the frailty of their faith, He reminded them of great victories from the past, such as the crossing of the Red Sea. Now, He said, greater things awaited.

Can you imagine how the true believers among God's people must have reacted to His promise? There was going to be a new thing—something entirely different from what had been seen before! The anticipation that must have gripped them was probably a little like the excitement on the faces of my grandchildren at Disneyland. The children were hopping up and down by the time we entered the park, where we were met by Mickey Mouse and Donald Duck. Then the train went by, chugging and blowing its whistle and ringing its bell. One event followed another, each one more exciting than the last. The children could hardly wait for what was just around the corner.

In a deeper and greater way, that is the spirit in which you can make this surrender to Christ. God is about to do a new thing in your life; what will He do next? How will He use you? In what new way will He reveal Himself to you? What precious new promises will you discover in His Word? What exciting answers to prayer will be yours?

When you come to the brink of this surrender and decide to dive in, be prepared for excitement. God is about to lead you into a whole new world. This sensible, living surrender is the bedrock step of faith that God can use to keep you from becoming a casualty. The path of sin and the lure of this world will seem dull compared to the joys of the surrendered life.

THE HOLY SPIRIT: OUR RESOURCE IN BATTLE

God has given a special resource to those who live under Christ's lordship. That resource is a Person: God's Holy Spirit.

The Holy Spirit helps us to battle the two primary forces of evil Satan uses to put us on the casualty list: false teachers outside and sin within.

When false teachers bring false doctrine, the Holy Spirit helps us sort out the false from the true: "Now we have received, not the spirit of the world, but the Spirit which is of God; that we might know the things that are freely given to us of God" (1 Cor. 2:12). We received the Holy Spirit if and when we turned to Christ in repentance and faith; the Spirit lives in us. As Paul wrote, "Know ye not that ye are the temple of God, and that the Spirit of God dwelleth in you?" (1 Cor. 3:16)

False teachers who harass us with false doctrine can be overcome by the wisdom and power of the Holy Spirit. If we can know the truth which comes from God, we will be able to discern what is false. That fact gives great comfort and assurance to anyone who desires to follow the Lord; in this life, phony road signs are not always easily spotted. That which is true often appears false and vice versa.

The Spirit of God helps us battle our own tendencies to sin. These are influences which, if left unchecked, can put us on the casualty list. Lust, pride, greed, covetousness, hate—such powerful enemies pose great danger to our spiritual welfare but can be overcome by the power of the Holy Spirit. He convicts us of our sin, opens the Word of God to us, and reveals to us the danger of harboring these deadly beasts in our hearts. "Wherewithall shall a young man cleanse his way?

By taking heed thereto according to Thy Word. . . . Thy Word have I hid in mine heart, that I might not sin against Thee" (Ps. 119:9, 11). Thus the Spirit shows us our sin and enables us to confess and find cleansing. "If we confess our sins, He is faithful and just to forgive us our sins, and to cleanse us from all unrighteousness" (1 John 1:9).

POWER AND PRESENCE

The Holy Spirit also ministers to us by infusing us with God's power and encouraging us with His presence. Paul speaks of this when writing to Timothy: "At my first answer no man stood with me, but all men forsook me: I pray God that it may not be laid to their charge. Notwithstanding the Lord stood with me, and strengthened me" (2 Tim. 4:16-17).

Paul was in Rome, on trial for his life. It was customary to allow a prominent man of high character to speak for the accused, plead his case, and arrange the evidence. But not a single person of this type had the courage to stand with Paul. He was abandoned by all, possibly because to stand with him would have been dangerous. This is what makes Paul's remark so meaningful; the Lord alone stood with Paul and infused him with His own power.

Both Old and New Testaments ring out the truth of God's strengthening presence with the believer. For example, "Fear thou not; for I am with thee: be not dismayed; for I am thy God: I will strengthen thee; yea, I will help thee; yea, I will uphold thee with the right hand of My righteousness. . . . For I the Lord thy God will hold thy right hand, saying unto thee, Fear not; I will help thee" (Isa. 41:10, 13).

The Lord wants to keep His people from becoming casualties; He quiets their fears and bolsters their faith. His promise is, "I will never leave thee, nor forsake thee" (Heb. 13:5).

When pressures threaten to crush our spirits, His Word reminds us, "It is of the Lord's mercies that we are not consumed, because His compassions fail not. They are new every morning: great is Thy faithfulness" (Lam. 3:22-23).

One of the clearest examples of God's abiding presence is His promise to those who want to witness for Him: "But when the Comforter is come, whom I will send unto you from the Father, even the Spirit of Truth, which proceedeth from the Father, He shall testify of Me: and ye also shall bear witness, because ye have been with Me from the beginning" (John 15:26-27).

Two are mentioned here: the believer and the Spirit of Truth (also referred to as the Comforter). *Comforter* is also translated as Counselor, Helper, Advocate, Intercessor, Strengthener. The word is *paraclete*—one who comes alongside to help. According to *An Expository Dictionary of New Testament Words* by W.E. Vine, the word "suggests the capability or adaptability for giving aid. It was used in a court of justice to denote a legal assistant, counsel for the defense." This, of course, was exactly what Paul did not have; the Lord became his advocate.

The Holy Spirit is the One who comes alongside to help. The moment you open your Bible and begin to tell someone about Christ, for example, the Holy Spirit begins to speak to that person as well—convicting him of his sin, revealing the perfect standard of righteousness that God demands, and warning him of the judgment to come. In other words, since Pentecost there has never really been a "one-on-one" witnessing situation. There is the person listening, the person speaking, and the Holy Spirit who comes alongside to help.

We can take comfort in the fact that when we surrender our lives to Christ, God provides the resource of His Spirit. By "coming alongside," the Spirit helps us to keep living the surrendered life and to keep off the casualty list.

We can agree quickly enough that to walk with Christ is the best thing we can do. We can readily agree that it is sensible, right, and obvious from Scripture. But one thing it is not: It is not easy. Not for me, anyway.

When I became a Christian, I told all my drinking buddies what I had done; I said I was going to wholly follow the Lord. They thought it was a bad idea. "After all," they argued, "all the fun will go out of your life." Looking back, I know they were wrong. But at the time I really had to fight it out with myself. *Would* I live a life stripped of fun, laughter, and good times? I had to tell God that if that was what it meant, I would press ahead anyhow. I made the surrender.

But surrendering didn't stop there. In the work to which God has called me there are new surrenders coming my way all the time. Frequently I am asked to go somewhere and preach, for example; on occasion two invitations for the same time will present a clear choice. One will be to a place overseas where the water is unsafe to drink, the food is often not very good, the mosquitoes are big enough to carry you off, the climate is hot and humid, the room is not air-conditioned, and the bed is a mat on the floor. The other invitation would take me to a place where the water is good, the food is familiar, the room is air-conditioned, and the bed is comfortable. How should I decide? On the basis of my own comfort? On the basis of which is easier? No. In every case I need to pray the simple prayer of Paul, "Lord, what wilt Thou have me to do?" (Acts 9:6)

I don't know what tests of Christ's lordship will come your way. But I know this: They will come. And when they do, you won't have to cave into temptation and become a casualty. Thanks to the promises and strengthening presence of God, you can respond with enthusiasm, faith, and the clear surrender of Mary: "Behold the handmaid of the Lord; be it unto me according to Thy word" (Luke 1:38).

Ten

DISCIPLINE

Most Christians I'd met were content to let the preacher do it all. There were notable exceptions, but most people in the little church my wife and I attended were perfectly willing to sit quietly and let the pastor do the job for which he'd been trained, and for which they were paying him. It was their job to back him, support him, pray for him, listen to him. He in turn studied the Bible and preached it, and shared the Gospel with non-Christians. He did it all, and he was good at it. I too assumed that was the way it should be.

But then I met a group of Christians, the Navigators, who seemed to say, "Not so!" It was their idea the *everyone*—pastor and people alike—should be "out in the battle." *Everyone* should be winning souls and studying and memorizing the Bible regularly. They quoted passages from the Old and New Testaments, lots of them, that seemed to back up their ideas.

As I got more and more involved with these people, I studied and memorized most of those passages. One illustrated their philosophy of life and ministry as well as any:

"They all hold swords, being expert in war: every man hath his sword upon his thigh because of fear in the night" (Song 3:8).

READY FOR BATTLE

I could see from verse 7 that this passage referred to "the valiant of Israel." These men had served with David; they were good soldiers with a heart for the battle, trained in the use of their weapons, disciplined, and single-minded (1 Chron. 12:33). The Navigators pointed out to me the words "all" and "every man." Not just a select few, but all who named the name of Christ were to be like that. Certainly the preacher should be, but just as certainly the men and women in the pew were to be too.

This is a fairly well accepted doctrine among most evangelicals these days, but back then it was a revolutionary thought. Back then, in the 1940s, the *preachers* were the "valiant men" of the faith; the lay people were a kind of backup team to help him do his job. He was the "expert" in the Word.

My Navigator friends saw the Bible as the Sword of the Spirit. They insisted that people in the pew also needed to be armed with the Word of God—to be able to use it to help others come to Christ and to grow. Most of all they needed to apply Scripture consistently to their own lives. Without a firsthand grasp of the Bible, Christians were easy prey for the world, the flesh, and the devil. It was all too easy for them to end up on the casualty list.

An experience I had in the Marine Corps in World War II reminds me of the need for such readiness in battle. Shortly after we hit the beach in the invasion of Peleliu, an artillery shell hit our armored amphibious tank broadside. Before we could react, another shell plowed into the 75mm ammo stacked along our port side. Needless to say, we all jumped out of the tank and began to make our way inland.

Soon the sergeant came to me and asked, "You OK, Eims?"

"Yeah," I replied, "I'm fine."

He looked at me. "Eims, where's your helmet?" he asked.

"Must be back in the tank, Sarge," I answered.

"How about your duty belt?"

"Back in the tank."

"As a matter of fact, Eims, where's your *rifle?*"

There I was, hopping from hole to hole, tree to tree, bush to bush, absolutely useless to the cause and helpless to defend myself. I'd left my weapons and protection behind. That was what those Navigators were trying to impress on me with their insistence on "all" and "every man" being equipped with the Word. They provided me with Bible studies, Bible reading plans, Scripture memory helps, and instruction on how to meditate on the Bible and apply it to my life.

Dawson Trotman spoke of key Scripture passages as arrows that were kept in the quiver of the heart—which the Holy Spirit could fit to the bow of our lips to pierce a soul for Christ. We were warned against relying on human wisdom and man-made argument; we were exhorted to fill our lives with the Word of God and place our confidence in it.

SEVEN QUALITIES OF THE WORD

Disciplining ourselves to read, study, memorize, and meditate on the Word of God is vital. Another passage that throws light on this fact is Psalm 19:7-11:

The Law of the Lord is perfect, converting the soul: the testimony of the Lord is sure, making wise the simple. The statutes of the Lord are right, rejoicing the heart:

the commandment of the Lord is pure, enlightening the eyes. The fear of the Lord is clean, enduring for ever: the judgments of the Lord are true and righteous altogether. More to be desired are they than gold, yea, than much fine gold: sweeter also than honey and the honeycomb. Moreover by them is Thy servant warned: and in keeping of them there is great reward.

Here the psalmist isolates seven attributes of the Word that make it required reading. Let's look at them one by one:

1. *The Bible is perfect.* Perfection is hard to attain, but God has done it in His Word. It is absolutely without blemish. The root of the word translated "perfect" also means complete, whole, and entire; we can add nothing to Scripture. Perfection needs no embellishment, no supplement. It is perfect as it stands.

This truth is sometimes ignored. I once heard a Christian leader say he advocated speaking in tongues because of the "imperfection" of the Bible. He cited 1 Corinthians 13:10: "But when that which is perfect is come, then that which is in part shall be done away." He claimed we are still waiting for God to complete His revelation—that the "perfect" has not come. Therefore God, through the gift of tongues, was continuing to add to His "imperfect" Word. Such nonsense! Such blasphemy! The Bible is the full, complete, whole, entire revelation from God.

It is through this Word that God calls us to repentance and faith in Christ, and by the power of the Holy Spirit "converts the soul." Peter reminds us that we are "born again, not of corruptible seed, but of incorruptible, by the Word of God, which liveth and abideth forever" (1 Peter 1:23). James says we must "receive with meekness the engrafted Word, which is able to save your souls" (James 1:21).

Once we are converted we find that the Word of God is

food for our souls. When we are down, it revives the inner life and restores our crumbling spirits.

2. *The Bible is "sure."* In an age of uncertainty, it is comforting to know the Bible is true. The root of the word translated "sure" conveys the idea of being permanent or verified. In the field of law, to verify means to affirm under oath. The writer of Hebrews mentions such verification:

> Wherein God, willing more abundantly to show unto the heirs of promise the immutability of His counsel, confirmed it by an oath: that by two immutable things, in which it was impossible for God to lie, we might have a strong consolation, who have fled for refuge to lay hold upon the hope set before us: which hope we have as an anchor of the soul, both sure and steadfast (Heb. 6:17-19).

According to John, these two "immutable things" are the person of Christ and the Word of Christ (Rev. 22:16, 18). Here we have the eternal God making a promise to His children, then swearing by an oath that He will keep that promise. To believe otherwise is to accuse God of perjury. He has anchored our hope in Jesus Christ and His Word.

To further verify all this, God "swore by Himself"—staked His reputation on it. He has anchored our faith so that when the winds of adversity, temptation, and affliction come, we can face them in confidence; His sure Word will keep us steadfast. We are fastened not to the shifting sands of this world, but to the sure promises of God.

3. *The Bible is "right, rejoicing the heart."* If you want to know and do what is right, and if you want the right answers to the riddles of life, turn to the Bible. The word for "right" conveys the idea of "straight," like a plumb line.

Many voices call us to adopt a particular lifestyle, to

accomplish some worldly goal, to achieve some earthly ambition. Many of these pursuits are quite attractive. But we must always measure them against the plumb line of God's Word; otherwise, our lives can end in sorrow and disaster on the casualty list. Paul chose that which would enable him to "finish my course with joy" (Acts 20:24). What a great thing to come to the end of life with a song on our lips and a smile on our faces! The Word can make the heart rejoice all the days of our lives.

4. *The Bible is pure.* It is not contaminated by anything foul. Nothing in it will make us spiritually sick.

One summer evening while my wife and I were traveling in Asia, we sat down to a meal in a small restaurant. When I bit into the meat, my teeth collided with a very hard object. Assuming it was simply unchewable gristle, I swallowed it whole and tried again. My next bite contained another rock-like obstacle; this time I took it out of my mouth with my fork and examined it.

It was a piece of glass about the size of a dime! Inspection revealed more glass on the meat. Apparently somebody in the kitchen had broken a bottle or dish and part of the glass had landed on my food. Thank God that His Word, food for our souls, contains no "foreign matter"—it's always absolutely pure. We can always feed on it with absolute confidence, knowing we will be "nourished up in the words of faith" because God's words are "wholesome" (1 Tim. 6:3).

5. *The Bible is clean.* This can also be translated as "radiant" or "bright." Of course! We would expect the Word to gleam with unequaled brilliance when we reflect on the words of John: "This then is the message which we have heard of Him, and declare unto you, that God is light, and in Him is no darkness at all" (1 John 1:5). If in God we find no darkness, we would fully expect His Word to shine too.

Have you even been on a dark path with a lantern or

flashlight that threw *some* light but not quite *enough?* The Bible will never let you down that way. The psalmist tells us, "Thy word is a lamp unto my feet, and a light unto my path" (Ps. 119:105).

To stumble along in the dark can be dangerous. When I was in high school, a bunch of us went out one night to steal watermelons. We were surprised by some adults who were waiting for us. I took off like a shot in the dark and almost killed myself, running smack into a neck-high clothesline that almost took my head off. I lay on the ground choking, coughing, trying to get my breath, until I finally recovered.

There is no need for a Christian to grope around in the dark, spiritually speaking. Get a good grasp on the Word and launch out in confidence. The Holy Spirit will use Scripture to keep you out of the ditch, on the right path, and off the casualty list.

6. *The Bible is "true and righteous altogether."* We would expect that, since the Scriptures have their origin in the Lord Himself. Make no mistake: Your Bible is the inspired Word of God. It crosses time and cultures; its message is for every generation, every age. You can stake your eternal soul and your daily life on it. Read it, hear it, study it, memorize it. That takes discipline, but it is worth every minute you invest.

THE DISCIPLINE OF PRAYER

Another discipline we must observe if we are to avoid being spiritually disabled is that of prayer. Even casual reading of the Bible shows the imperative of prayer as a daily discipline. The Lord Jesus is our prime example; one incident in His life is especially instructive for those of us who want to deepen our prayer lives:

"And He came out, and went, as He was wont, to the mount of Olives; and His disciples also followed Him. And when He was at the place, He said unto them, 'Pray that ye enter not into temptation.' And He was withdrawn from them about a stone's cast, and kneeled down, and prayed" (Luke 22:39-41).

Three things stand out in this passage:

1. *For Jesus, prayer was a consistent practice.* Luke says it was His custom. All too often we are just the opposite; our prayer lives are marked by inconsistency. We need to heed Paul's admonition to "Continue in prayer" (Col. 4:2). The idea is to hold on *with strength* so that this discipline won't be dropped.

It is easy to let this discipline slip. My wife Virginia is a tremendous challenge to me in this regard. Over the Christmas holidays one year, when our home was blessed with lots of visitors, my wife rose early and went to the kitchen table where she usually reads her Bible and daily devotional books. Her standard practice was to then go to an empty bedroom to pray, but the bedroom was occupied. So she went to my study. But soon I needed the study for some work, so she went to our bedroom—which was now empty. It would have been easy for her to make an excuse to drop her time with the Lord, but she didn't. She held on tight even though it was inconvenient.

2. *Jesus came to "the place" of prayer.* It's a good idea to have a regular place to pray. You can keep there what you need for your time with the Lord: Bible, prayer list, devotional books, and a notebook to record answers to prayer.

There is something special about a place that is set aside as holy, dedicated to the Lord. The Holy Spirit makes the place a special sanctuary for daily fellowship with God. Having a regular place can help you focus on your objective and keep your mind off sidetracks; when your mind drifts and you begin to think of something else, jot that concern in your notebook and get back to prayer. If you don't have a place of prayer, establish one and use it consistently.

3. *Jesus was dedicated to prayer.* He went to the place and prayed even though He knew being there would cost Him His life. Judas knew right where to find Him. He had seen Jesus pray there time and time again. All Jesus had to do was forgo His practice and place of prayer, and Judas would not have been able to locate Him.

This commitment unto death is reminiscent of an incident in the life of Daniel. A law had been passed, declaring "that whosoever shall ask a petition of any God or man for thirty days, save of thee, O King, shall be cast into the den of lions" (Dan. 6:7). Did this decree have any effect on Daniel? Did he agree to forgo his prayertime for thirty days? Hardly. "Now when Daniel knew that the writing was signed, he went into his house; and his windows being open in his chamber toward Jerusalem, he kneeled upon his knees three times a day, and prayed, and gave thanks before God, as he did aforetime" (Dan. 6:10).

Did the prayer life of Jesus have an effect on the apostles who walked with Him? Yes! Their commitment was, "We will give ourselves continually to prayer, and to the ministry of the Word" (Acts 6:4). His consistency led to theirs.

If you haven't done so already, may I suggest that you make a commitment by God's grace and with His help, to pray consistently? A commitment like this does two things: It conveys your determination to improve your prayer life, and admits total reliance on the grace of God to make it happen.

There is one other benefit of a disciplined prayer life, and it's often overlooked. As we observe over the years which prayers God says yes to and which He says no to, we learn about His character. For instance, an uncaring man or woman might allow a child to play on a heavily traveled boulevard—but a loving father or mother would not. God says no to our requests for things that would harm us; these acts of denial display His love and concern. This explains why John says, "And this is the confidence that we have in Him, that, if we ask any thing according to His will, He heareth us: and if we know that He hear us, whatsoever we ask, we know that we have the petitions that we desired of Him" (1 John 5:14-15).

DISCIPLINE PREVENTS DISABILITY

Over the years I have sadly watched many good men and women drop out of the battle and onto the casualty list. They have stopped pressing on and have caved in to the allurements of the world—the deceitfulness of riches, the promise of an easier life, the subtlety of self-centeredness, and countless other illusions. But one thing stands out loud and clear: I have never seen a person leave the battle as long as he or she wanted Christ as the center of life and bolstered that desire through the daily disciplines of Bible intake and prayer.

Invariably when I ask a "fallen soldier" how he fell, he will describe how he first became unfaithful in morning prayer and Bible reading. After that, he will confess, it was fairly easy to let go of Bible study and Scripture memorization. Then attendance at church became sporadic. Eventually his spiritual disability was complete.

Don't let that happen to you. God can use these disciplines in the basics to keep you fired up and on the active list. As you develop consistency and discipline in your walk with Christ, there will be ups and downs—especially at first. But don't let periodic failures deter you in your efforts. Nothing really important was ever achieved without dedication and struggle. With Paul, let us press on toward "the prize of the high calling of God in Christ Jesus" (Phil. 3:14).

Eleven

OUTREACH

Go on. Take another look up and down your street. What do you see? Houses? Cars? Vans? Trees? Condos? Apartments?

What are the *people* on your street doing? If it's early Sunday morning, when all those Gospel programs are on TV, the people are probably sleeping. If it's 11 o'clock, when church bells are ringing and greeters wait at the open church doors to offer warm welcomes, your neighbors are probably reading the Sunday paper. They're enjoying a second cup of coffee. Some of the more ambitious souls are washing their cars, cutting their lawns, or shoveling snow—depending on the season.

As you observe all this, you ask yourself the familiar questions: What's to be done? These people need to hear the Gospel, but how? They sleep when the TV gives the message; they do other things when the church opens its doors.

What's the answer? Better yet *who's* the answer?

You are.

Just as devotion and discipline are necessary to keep us off the casualty list, we need to keep reaching out with the

Gospel to stay vital. In this spiritual war God's kingdom must gain ground, not simply hold it. So let's look at that responsibility in this chapter. Let's take it beyond exhortations to bear witness, share a word of testimony, pass out a Gospel tract, or invite someone to church. Let's look at outreach in depth.

A CROWD OF WITNESSES

The Great Commission of Jesus Christ (Matt. 28:19-20) has a twofold thrust: evangelism and edification. We are to win the lost and build up the saved. As these two ministries mesh into a single vision, multiplication results. People are not only won to Christ but are also trained to walk with Him; in time they repeat that process in others' lives. It's a simple idea, but one that has tremendous potential for the spread of the Gospel. It's also an idea that has blossomed only recently in the minds of many who are concerned about world evangelization.

Dawson Trotman, founder of The Navigators, was used by the Lord to make the Christian world aware of this dynamic, one-two punch. Daws lived in an era when the Christian world was blessed with a host of amazingly gifted, fruitful evangelists who brought thousands to Christ through city-wide crusades at home and abroad. They were men like Jack Wyrtzen, Torrey Johnson, Merv Rosell, John R. Rice, Dr. Bob Jones, Sr., Percy Crawford, Chuck Templeton, T.W. Wilson, Grady Wilson, Billy Graham, and Dr. Hyman Appleman—to name just a few. Daws knew many of these men, applauded their efforts, and was himself a fruitful witness. But as he grew in the Lord and studied God's Word, he began to get an idea.

A phrase from Scripture came to his mind time and again; God was speaking to him, showing him something that seemed radical and fresh. He was to be fruitful, but there was more. He was to be fruitful—*and multiply*, spiritually speaking.

Here was a way for the "ordinary" believer to have a significant impact on his or her world for Christ. If every Christian could engage in a "multiplying ministry," a vast, untapped resource could be used by the Holy Spirit to bring thousands to Christ. The efforts of the gifted evangelists could be supplemented by the straightforward, clear witness of millions of ordinary people.

Do you see the potential power of all this? One Navigator staff member expressed it memorably when he held up an apple and asked how many seeds were in it. Then he held up one apple seed and asked a more profound question: How many apples were in that one seed? What a question! There were potentially hundreds, thousands, millions!

The potential of one fruitful and multiplying layman is staggering. Just as there are millions of apples in a tiny seed, there are millions of souls waiting to be born into the kingdom of God through your life and ministry.

Do you need to broaden the picture you have of yourself? Maybe you see yourself as a person who can help the pastor do *his* job. That's fair enough; you should, because he needs your help. But God sees in you much more. He sees you as a "good seed" whom He can use to bring forth much fruit. Yes, you—not just the supertalented, not just those with the "gift of gab" and a "way with people." If you believe otherwise, you have in effect put *yourself* on the casualty list—and that's a double tragedy.

ELEVEN KEYS TO EVANGELISM

Let's step back into your neighborhood for a moment. All those people there—lost, indifferent to spiritual matters, complacent, self-satisfied. How do you enter their lives and bring them to Christ?

I recently heard Dave Cauwells, a businessman from Albuquerque, tell a group what he had learned about witnessing to his friends, neighbors, and business associates. He mentioned eleven points that are worth taking to heart:

1. *You've got to* want *to witness.* I believe the average layman needs to be fixed up, freed up, and fired up if he is to be effective for Christ. To get fixed up, he needs to confess his sins, get his priorities straight, and make Christ Lord. To be freed up, he needs to be able to articulate the Gospel and be familiar with the rest of the Word of God. To be fired up, he must have a desire to see people come to Christ. If he has little desire to share the Gospel, he may need to meditate on the following Scripture passages:

When I say unto the wicked, "Thou shalt surely die"; and thou givest him not warning, nor speakest to warn the wicked from his wicked way, to save his life; the same wicked man shall die in his iniquity; but his blood will I require at thine hand. Yet if thou warn the wicked, and he turn not from his wickedness, nor from his wicked way, he shall die in his iniquity; but thou hast delivered thy soul (Ezek. 3:18-19).

If thou forbear to deliver them that are drawn unto death, and those that are ready to be slain; if thou sayest, "Behold, we knew it not"; doth not He that pondereth the heart consider it? And He that keepeth thy soul, doth not He know it? And shall not He render to every man according to his works? (Prov. 24:11-12)

2. *Be yourself.* Don't try to be a copy of another Christian. Let God use *you.*

3. *Have a daily quiet time.* Why? Because, in the words of Christ, "I am the Vine, ye are the branches: He that abideth in Me, and I in him, the same bringeth forth much fruit: for without Me ye can do nothing" (John 15:5).

4. *Study the Word.* The message of the Gospel is in the Bible. The answers to your neighbor's doubts and fears are in the Bible. To be a good witness, you need to have a good grasp of the Scriptures.

5. *Pray for specific non-Christians by name.* Day by day, pray up and down the street. Pray for opportunities to get to know your neighbors, to be able to do them a favor, to one day share the Gospel.

6. *Try to relate to them.* Don't isolate yourself. Join a club; join a health spa; try to find a commonality. Pass the word up and down your street that you're holding a get-acquainted cookout—that you'll furnish the charcoal and cooking facilities if each neighbor brings his own salad and steak. Some will come, you'll meet them, and the next contact will be a bit easier.

7. *Be interested in them.* After you've met your neighbors, go and see their flower gardens, their boats, their home movies, whatever.

8. *Meet them at a point of need.* Take a casserole over if one of your neighbors is sick. Offer to watch his kids. Try to be a friend.

9. *Know how to share your faith.* Use a method with which you are familiar. The Navigators publish a booklet, *The Bridge to Life,* that many have found helpful in this regard; other booklets and programs are also available through your church or bookstore.

10. *After you have shared the Gospel with your neighbor, ask him or her to accept Christ.* Use simple questions such as, "Now that you have heard the message, is there any reason you couldn't accept Christ right now?"

11. *Follow-up with the new Christian.* Get him or her into a Bible study, a Sunday School class, a good church.

THE IMPORTANCE OF FOLLOW-UP

That eleventh key, follow-up, is extremely important. You are to be fruitful *and* multiply; follow-up is the first step in multiplication. As your neighbor begins to grow and learns how to tell others about the Lord, he or she will have a circle of friends to lead to Christ—who in turn can repeat the process among *their* friends. Soon you will have spiritual children, grandchildren, and so on all over the place.

Follow-up is also crucial because those who can do the most damage to the cause of Christ are those who claim to be Christians but don't live the life. Through your follow-up, the Holy Spirit can mold people into the image and likeness of Christ—and keep them off the casualty list as well.

To follow up effectively, you must be willing to share your life with others. As indicated by Paul in 1 Thessalonians 1:5-10:

For our Gospel came not unto you in word only, but also in power, and in the Holy Ghost, and in much assurance; as ye know what manner of men we were among you for your sake. And ye became followers of us, and of the Lord, having received the Word in much affliction, with joy of the Holy Ghost: so that ye were examples to all that believe in Macedonia and Achaia. For from you sounded out the Word of the Lord not only in Macedonia and Achaia, but also in every place your faith to God-ward is spread abroad; so that we need not to speak any thing. For they themselves show of us what manner of entering in we had unto you, and how ye turned to God from idols to serve the living and true God; and to wait for his Son from heaven, whom he raised from the dead, even Jesus, which delivered us from the wrath to come.

Paul preached the Gospel to the Thessalonians; in time, these new Christians passed the message along to the people in Macedonia and Achaia. But it didn't just "happen." Paul had to spend personal time with these people ("every one of you")—encouraging, comforting, and urging them to live lives worthy of God (1 Thes. 2:11-12).

As you become involved in the lives of others, your heart and mind are set on the right things. One of the key ways to stay off the casualty list is to be deeply involved in ministry to others. This is not to say that *busyness* is the solution; it is not. Quiet times of reflection on the Lord are imperative. But involvement in the lives of others keeps our minds set on the "right stuff." As Paul wrote, "This I say then, Walk in the Spirit, and ye shall not fulfill the lust of the flesh" (Gal. 5:16).

Move ahead in the things of God. As long as an airplane in flight moves ahead at the proper speed, its lift is greater than the pull of gravity. Similarly, to stay off the spiritual scrap heap, we must keep fighting and have our minds occupied with the Lord and the work He has called us to do.

Twelve

OBEDIENCE

For three years our electric teakettle had served us well. Then one day we plugged it in and nothing happened. So I took it to the repair shop, where the lady asked, "What's wrong with it?"

"It doesn't work," I replied.

She took the cord, plugged it into a gadget, and said, "I think it's the cord." She got a new cord, attached it to the kettle, and plugged it into the gadget. A light went on. "You need a new cord," she said.

I bought the cord, came home, filled the teakettle, plugged it in, and lo and behold—the water began to boil! I threw away the old cord and fixed my wife Virginia a cup of coffee and myself a cup of tea.

What happened to that kettle can happen to the believer. If the "power connection" between God and the disciple is broken, nothing happens. God cannot use that Christian to accomplish His work on earth. Spiritual needs go unmet; lost souls continue to languish in their sin. Eventually the disciple's heart grows cold, and the Lord has to set that person aside and get someone else to do His bidding. The "disconnected" Christian has become a casualty.

What has broken that vital connection? Disobedience to the Word of God. As long as the disciple walks in obedience, all's well. When he disobeys, he "pulls the plug" from his end.

WHAT DOES GOD WANT?

Obedience to the Word of God is a concept that's often misunderstood. What is it that God really wants? I'm afraid many people who think they are on the right track are really headed in the wrong direction.

Take, for instance, a group of people I met a few years ago. I had been asked to preach in their church. When I arrived I found some of them wearing large, round badges. The badges indicated that their wearers regularly attended about half dozen meetings at the church each week.

As I talked with the badge-wearers, it became apparent that they were quite satisfied with themselves. They perceived themselves as being the good guys, the backbone of the church. The people without badges, however, weren't so confident. Feeling that they didn't "measure up," they were somewhat intimidated by the badge-wearers.

As I watched that little drama being played out that night, I wondered whether the "badgers" were really doing what the Lord wanted. It was clear by the way they strutted around, looked down their noses at the "non-badgers," and wore self-satisfied smiles that they thought they were pleasing God. But was coming within earshot of half a dozen religious talks each week the end of it? Is that what puts a person in good graces with God? As long as your eardrums vibrate with the sound of Scripture, are you on track? Is that what Jesus said?

I am not against attending church meetings. I love going to

church; our family attends morning and evening worship and Sunday School every week. I sincerely enjoy hearing the Word of God expounded. But is that all there is?

IS UNDERSTANDING ENOUGH?

I've met a second group that goes beyond the "badgers." This second group would say, "Yes, hearing the Word is good. But there is another step. We must hear *and understand* it."

With this group there is a keen satisfaction in being exposed to what they call "the meat of the Word." Each Sunday their pastor takes out his overhead projector and shows the transparencies he has prepared in multiple colors as he teaches the passage. He does it verse by verse—no topical sermon for this group! They want the Bible taught "just as it was written"—verse by verse, chapter by chapter, book by book, week after week, year after year.

The longer you go to this church, the more you "understand." You understand the tenses of the Greek verbs and how they throw new light on everything. You understand what names like Paul and Saul and Peter mean. Obscure passages are "explained" as clearly as if they were John 3:16. For this group, to *understand* is to be on the inside track with God.

Let me hasten to say that I am all for understanding the Word. In fact, Jesus taught, "But he that received seed into the good ground is he that heareth the Word, and understandeth it; which also beareth fruit, and bringeth forth, some an hundredfold, some sixty, some thirty" (Matt. 13:23).

Just as our first group was not doing wrong when it spent many hours in hearing the Word, our second group is certainly doing well when it hungers and thirsts for a clear understanding of the Word. We can look at that group and say, "Keep it up! More power to you!" But is *that* all there is to obedience?

IS TEACHING THE ANSWER?

There is a third group that goes a step further. Its members applaud those who hear the Word; they praise those who desire to understand the Word. "But," this group adds, "the key is to be able to *explain* the Word of God to *others.*"

It's true that nothing is really yours until you can give it away. It's especially true with Scripture. When you study a passage, the clearest evidence that you truly understand it is your ability to explain it to someone else.

Therefore, the third group contends, the emphasis must be on helping people become teachers of the Word. To become a Bible teacher is the chief good. If this church, Sunday School class, seminary, or other organization is producing teachers of the Word, it believes it is doing the thing God wants. After all, if a good Bible teacher expounds the Word clearly, won't the lives of his listeners be changed? Won't they become better people, more loving, kind, generous, joyful, thankful? And isn't that the point of it all—changed lives?

DOERS OF THE WORD

As you ponder all this, you may feel a bit confused. You may find yourself agreeing with all three groups. After all, when a preacher gives the Sunday morning announcements, doesn't he exhort people to come to the next meeting *whatever* it is? "Come and hear the Word," he may say. And what could be wrong with understanding the Bible or being able to teach it clearly to others? Perhaps you would vote for all three approaches. But before you cast your vote, consider the words of Jesus as recorded in Luke 6:47-49:

> Whosoever cometh to Me, and heareth My sayings, and doeth them, I will show you to whom he is like: He is like a man which built an house, and digged deep, and laid the foundation on a rock: and when the flood arose, the stream beat vehemently upon that house, and could not shake it: for it was founded upon a rock. But he that heareth, and doeth not, is like a man that without a foundation built an house upon the earth; against which the stream did beat vehemently, and immediately it fell; and the ruin of that house was great.

This is a story of two builders. Both worked hard; both perspired in the midday sun. There is no evidence that one house was larger or fancier than the other. Yet one came to disaster and the other didn't. Why? Because one had a solid foundation and the other did not.

Jesus said this was a picture of two lives—one ruined, another strong and enduring. The difference was in their responses to the Word. Both heard, but only the one who heard and *obeyed* was to be commended.

To hear, understand, and teach is good. But to *do* is imperative. To *not* do will bring us to ruin—no matter how much we "know."

In John 14:6 Jesus is seen to be the only way to eternal bliss in the hereafter. In the "two houses" passage Jesus implies that obedience to His Word is the only way to a happy life in the here and now. The casualty list awaits the one who persistently disobeys.

Do. What a small word to carry such *gigantic* consequences. No wonder Jesus emphasized this truth time and again:

Then came to Him His mother and His brethren, and could not come at Him for the press. And it was told Him by certain which said, "Thy mother and Thy brethren stand without, desiring to see Thee." And He answered and said unto them, "My mother and My brethren are these which hear the Word of God, and do it" (Luke 8:19-21).

And it came to pass, as He spake these things, a certain woman of the company lifted up her voice, and said unto Him, "Blessed is the womb that bare Thee, and the paps which Thou hast sucked." But He said, "Yea rather, blessed are they that hear the Word of God, and keep it" (Luke 11:27-28).

What Jesus is saying is clear: If you are a Christian, live like one.

In Colorado Springs where I live, a sports channel is available on television. One Saturday morning I turned to that channel, hoping to watch tennis or golf. I was surprised to see a program called "Legends of Pool."

Legends of pool? I thought. I'd heard of programs featuring legends of golf like Arnold Palmer, or legends of tennis like Bill Tilden—but never "Legends of Pool." I was intrigued. Who were these legends?

As I watched, I found that they were old-timers with names like Luther Lassiter, E.J. Puckett, Rags Woods, and Minnesota Fats. When the time came for Rags Woods to shoot, the announcer said this legend had been placed in an impossible position. The ball he was supposed to hit just couldn't be hit. The commentator went on and on describing the tragedy of the situation; apparently Woods' inability to hit the ball would cost him hundreds of dollars in prize money.

It was all over, the announcer declared. Rags had lost. But old Rags just kept walking around the table, examining the situation. You could almost hear his brain at work, recalling thousands of pool games over scores of years. A quiet smile came to his face as he finally bent over the table, took careful aim, and shot. Various balls went in all directions. But he hit the ball he was supposed to be unable to hit, and it went straight into the pocket!

The announcer went wild. Rags had done it! He had made an "absolutely impossible" shot. Rags, on the other hand, didn't seem surprised at all. I said to myself, *That's right. When I am watching a legend, I expect him to act like a legend.*

In a sense, that's what Jesus is saying. If you claim to be a Christian, live like one. If you call Jesus Lord, do what He says.

HANDS-ON EXPERIENCE

Dawson Trotman devised an illustration to show how to get a grasp on the Word of God. He called it the Hand Illustration because it used the fingers and thumb to represent ways of appropriating the Word into our lives. The little finger stood for hearing the Word, the ring finger for reading the Word, the middle for Bible Study, the index finger for Scripture memorization, and the thumb for meditating on the Word. Five passages of Scripture show the *purpose* of all this hearing, reading, and so on:

Hearing: "But be ye doers of the Word, and not hearers only, deceiving your own selves" (James 1:22).

Reading: "And it shall be with him, and he shall read therein all the days of his life: that he may learn to fear the Lord his God, to keep all the words of this law and these statutes, to do them" (Deut. 17:19).

Study: "My son, if thou wilt receive my words, and hide my commandments with thee; so that thou incline thine ear unto wisdom, and apply thine heart to understanding; yea, if thou criest after knowledge, and liftest up thy voice for understanding; if thou seekest her as silver, and searchest for her as for hid treasures; then shalt thou understand the fear of the Lord, and find the knowledge of God. . . . That thou mayest walk in the way of good men, and keep the paths of the righteous" (Prov. 2:1-5, 20).

Memorizing: "But the Word is very nigh unto thee, in thy mouth, and in thy heart, that thou mayest do it" (Deut. 30:14).

Meditating: "This Book of the Law shall not depart out of thy mouth; but thou shalt meditate therein day and night, that thou may observe to do according to all that is written therein: for then thou shalt make thy way prosperous, and then thou shalt have good success" (Josh. 1:8).

Notice the connecting thread: The purpose of biblical intake is that we may *do* it, *obey* it, *keep* it. To fall short of this is to miss the point of believing the Bible in the first place.

An article published by Wycliffe Bible Translators reported that Moran, Chief of the Piro Tribe of jungle Indians of western South America, said, "When my wife does something wrong, I say to her, 'Nina, God's Word says so-and-so.' And she says, "Moran, is that what God's Word says?" So I give her the Word and she reads it for herself and then she doesn't do that anymore. When I do something I shouldn't, she says to me soft and meek like she always is, 'Moran, doesn't God's Word say so-and-so?' So then I go and read it and by God's help I don't do that anymore."

Isn't that dynamite? If every believer around the world were as committed to obeying Scripture as Moran and Nina are, the church would be revived, the lives of believers sanctified, and the world evangelized. Much has been written and said about evangelism as a lifestyle, but that will never happen until *obedience* becomes a lifestyle. To be effective witnesses we must be filled with the Holy Spirit, and the Spirit does not control a person who is living in disobedience to the Word of God.

The Apostle Paul stresses the necessity of obedience in his letter to the Romans:

> By whom we have received grace and apostleship, for obedience to the faith among all nations, for His name (Rom. 1:5).

> Now to Him that is of power to stablish you according to my Gospel, and the preaching of Jesus Christ, according to the revelation of the mystery, which was kept secret since the world began, but now is made manifest, and by the Scriptures of the prophets, according to the commandment of the everlasting God, made known to all nations for the obedience of faith (Rom. 16:25-26).

THE DANGER OF DISOBEDIENCE

Our Lord wants disciples who are faithful unto death, lifetime laborers in the work of His kingdom. Obeying Him is the primary key to staying on His active list. How can He guide us if we are living contrary to His will? How can He bless our lives if we are disobeying Him? But if He finds us pressing toward the prize of the high calling of God in Jesus Christ, His Spirit will be mightily at work in our lives, enabling us to withstand the world, the flesh, and the devil. Not only will we keep off the casualty list—we will charge ahead with the joy and confidence the Spirit inspires.

As Paul points out, there is real danger to the active

Christian: "I therefore so run, not as uncertainly; so fight I, not as one that beateth the air: but I keep under my body, and bring it into subjection: lest that by any means, when I have preached to others, I myself should be a castaway" (1 Cor. 9:26-27). Think of it! The great apostle himself was concerned that he might cave in somewhere along the way. Later in that same letter he warned, "Wherefore let him that thinketh he standeth take heed lest he fall" (1 Cor. 10:12).

Recently I was praying earnestly for my own life in this regard. The Holy Spirit had reminded me that men and women who were far more godly, more dedicated, and more fruitful than I am have quit the battle. Some have fallen to the allurements of the world, some to the corruptions of their own fleshly desires, and some to the wiles of the devil. It would serve little purpose for me to list case histories; you've seen it happen too and are no doubt grieved as well. Such tragedies remind us to, in the words of Paul, take heed to ourselves—to watch out, beware.

FOR THOSE ON THE CASUALTY LIST

I hope that you are not among the spiritually disabled. But what if you are? What can a person do if he has left the battlefield and is now languishing by the wayside?

There is hope. If you're on the casualty list and want to be "reactivated," I would suggest the following:

1. *Go to someone who is "pressing on" and ask for help.* Possibly that person would meet with you from time to time to encourage you, help you back on to your feet, and get you pointed in the right direction again.

2. *Ask that person to pray for you.* Remember, "The effectual fervent prayer of a righteous man availeth much" (James 5:16).

3. *Ask the Lord for strength and courage to begin again.*

Remember, it's always too soon to quit—and it's never too late to begin again. God is far more interested in your getting back on track than you are; He will be right there to help. He is waiting for you to reach out, and His strong arm is ready to take hold and strengthen you.

4. *Get into the Word.* Remember the prayer of Jesus: "Sanctify them through Thy truth: Thy word is truth" (John 17:17). The Spirit of God can use the Bible to encourage, guide, strengthen, and motivate you to get out of the ditch, dust yourself off, and get back into the battle.

5. *Don't expect to be able to do too much too soon.* Your weakened "prayer legs" will not support a hearty, robust prayer life at first. Your capacity for the Word may have shrunk temporarily. You may be vulnerable to some temptation that will continue to plague you for a while. Don't be discouraged. Nothing of worth comes easy. Set your jaw and pledge, "By the grace of God I will come back!"

6. *Remember that you are a child of God and victory is rightfully yours.* Trust God to give it to you. Claim 1 Corinthians 15:57: "But thanks be to God, which giveth us the victory through our Lord Jesus Christ."

Yes, you may stumble and fall again. But don't just lie there! Paul spoke of being "cast down, but not destroyed" (2 Cor. 4:9). J.B. Phillips puts it, "We may be knocked down but we are never knocked out!" That, thank the Lord, is the heritage of every child of God.

May God give us grace to keep pressing on in this spiritual war. Because of Christ, the kingdom's victory is ultimately assured. If we stay close to Him, the triumph will be ours as well.